STEP-BY-STEP
bread

STEP-BY-STEP
bread

Caroline Bretherton

LONDON, NEW YORK,
MUNICH, MELBOURNE, DELHI

Editorial Assistant David Fentiman
Senior Editor Alastair Laing
Project Art Editor Kathryn Wilding
Senior Art Editor Sara Robin
Managing Editor Dawn Henderson
Managing Art Editor Christine Keilty
Senior Jacket Creative Nicola Powling
Production Editor Siu Chan
Production Controller Claire Pearson
Creative Technical Support Sonia Charbonnier
Photographers Howard Shooter, Michael Hart

DK INDIA
Assistant Editor Ekta Sharma
Designer Divya PR
Managing Editor Glenda Fernandes
Managing Art Editor Navidita Thapa
DTP Manager Sunil Sharma
DTP Operator Rajdeep Singh

First published in Great Britain in 2012
by Dorling Kindersley Limited
80 Strand, London WC2R 0RL

Penguin Group (UK)

2 4 6 8 10 9 7 5 3 1
001 – 180674 – May/2012

Copyright © 2012 Dorling Kindersley Limited

All rights reserved. No part of this publication
may be reproduced, stored in a retrieval system,
or transmitted in any form or by any means,
electronic, mechanical, photocopying, recording,
or otherwise without the prior written permission
of the copyright owners.

A CIP catalogue record for this book
is available from the British Library

ISBN 978-1-4053-6825-4

Colour reproduction by
Media Development Printing Ltd, UK

Printed and bound in Singapore by Tien Wah Press

Discover more at www.dk.com

Contents

Breakfast

RECIPE CHOOSERS

Buttermilk Biscuits
page 130

10 MINS 15 MINS

Pane al latte
page 164

30 MINS 20 MINS

American Blueberry Pancakes page 132

10 MINS 15–20 MINS

Banana, Yogurt, and Honey Pancake Stack page 136

10 MINS 15–20 MINS

Croissants
page 176

1 HOUR 15–20 MINS

Croissants aux amandes
page 179

1 HOUR 15–20 MINS

Danish Pastries
page 180

30 MINS 15–20 MINS

Almond Crescents
page 182

30 MINS 15–20 MINS

Apricot Pastries
page 183

30 MINS 15–20 MINS

Bagels page 50

40 MINS 25–25 MINS

Pains au chocolat
page 178

1 HOUR 15–20 MINS

Multi-grain Breakfast Bread
page 36

45–50 MINS 40–45 MINS

Afternoon Tea

Bara Brith
page 170

40 MINS   25–40 MINS

English Muffins
page 30

25–30 MINS   13–16 MINS

Cinnamon Rolls
page 172

40 MINS   25–30 MINS

Oatcakes
page 114

20 MINS   15 MINS

Crumpets
page 138

10 MINS   20–26 MINS

Hot Crossed Buns
page 175

30 MINS   15–20 MINS

Brioche Buns
page 158

40–50 MINS   15–20 MINS

Chelsea Buns
page 174

30 MINS   30 MINS

A Meal In Itself

Four Seasons Pizza
page 82

40 MINS   40 MINS

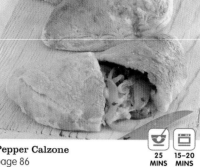

Pepper Calzone
page 86

25 MINS   15–20 MINS

Pissaladière
page 88

20 MINS   1 HOUR 25 MINS

Stuffed Paratha
page 100

20 MINS   15–20 MINS

Quesadillas
page 104

5–10 MINS   30–35 MINS

Spiced Lamb Pies
page 94

40–45 MINS   10–15 MINS

Staffordshire Oatcakes
page 144

10 MINS   15 MINS

Buckwheat Galettes page 142

25 MINS   25–30 MINS

Zweibelkuchen
page 90

30 MINS   60–65 MINS

With Drinks

Ciabatta Crostini
page 42

15 MINS   10 MINS

Grissini
page 106

40-45 MINS   15-18 MINS

Parmesan and Rosemary Thins page 112

10 MINS   15 MINS

Pita Crisps
page 95

10 MINS   7-8 MINS

Blinis
page 146

20 MINS   15 MINS

Prawn and Guacamole Tortilla Stacks page 105

15 MINS   10-15 MINS

Cheese Straws
page 113

10 MINS   15 MINS

Pretzels
page 54

50 MINS   20 MINS

Stilton and Walnut Biscuits
page 110

10 MINS   20 MINS

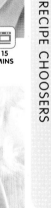

Parma Ham-wrapped Canapés page 109

45 MINS   15-18 MINS

Daily Breads

RECIPE CHOOSERS

Wholemeal Cottage Loaf
page 16

35–40 MINS   40–45 MINS

White Loaf
page 20

20 MINS   40–45 MINS

Ciabatta
page 40

30 MINS   30 MINS

Pan al latte
page 164

30 MINS   20 MINS

Pane siciliano
page 76

20 MINS   25–30 MINS

Quick Pumpkin Bread
page 122

20 MINS   50 MINS

Artisan Rye Bread
page 72

25 MINS   40–50 MINS

Pumpernickel
page 75

20 MINS   30–40 MINS

Sourdough Loaf
page 63

45–50 MINS   40–45 MINS

Rosemary Focaccia
page 46
30–35 MINS 15–20 MINS

Walnut and Rosemary Loaf
page 21
20 MINS 30–40 MINS

Wholmeal Baguette
page 71
20 MINS 20–25 MINS

Challah
page 163
45–55 MINS 35–40 MINS

Cornbread
page 126
15–20 MINS 20–25 MINS

Anadama Cornbread
page 38
25 MINS 45–50 MINS

Soda Bread
page 118
10–15 MINS 35–40 MINS

Hefezopf
page 160
20 MINS 25–35 MINS

classic breads

Wholemeal Cottage Loaf

Stone-ground wholemeal flour can vary in its absorbency, and you may need more or less flour and water.

MAKES 2 LOAVES | 35–40 MINS | 40–45 MINS | UP TO 8 WEEKS

Rising and proving time
1¾–2¼ hrs

Ingredients
60g (2oz) unsalted butter, plus extra for greasing
3 tbsp honey
3 tsp dried yeast
1 tbsp salt
625g (1lb 6oz) stone-ground strong wholemeal bread flour
125g (4½oz) strong white bread flour, plus extra for dusting

1 Melt the butter. Mix 1 tablespoon of honey and 4 tablespoons lukewarm water in a bowl.

2 Sprinkle the yeast over the honey mixture. Leave it for 5 minutes to dissolve, stirring once.

3 Mix the butter, yeast, salt, remaining honey, and 400ml (14fl oz) lukewarm water.

4 Stir in half the wholemeal flour with the white flour, and mix it with your hands.

5 Add the remaining wholemeal flour, 125g (4½oz) at a time, mixing after each addition.

6 The dough should be soft and slightly sticky, and pull away from the sides of the bowl.

7 Turn the dough out onto a floured work surface, and sprinkle it with white flour.

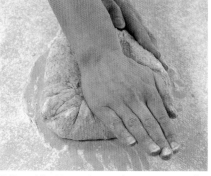

8 Knead for 10 minutes until it is very smooth, elastic, and forms a ball.

9 Grease a large bowl with butter. Put in the dough and flip it to butter the surface lightly.

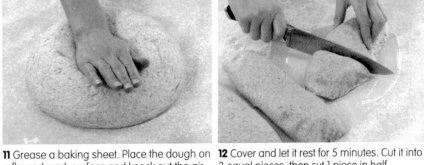

10 Cover with a damp tea towel. Leave it in a warm place for 1–1½ hours until doubled.

11 Grease a baking sheet. Place the dough on a floured work surface and knock out the air.

12 Cover and let it rest for 5 minutes. Cut it into 3 equal pieces, then cut 1 piece in half.

13 Cover 1 large and 1 small piece of dough with a tea towel, and shape the rest.

14 Shape 1 large piece into a loose ball. Fold in the sides, turn, and pinch to make a tight ball.

15 Flip the ball, seam side down, onto the prepared baking sheet.

16 Similarly, shape 1 small piece into a ball. Set it, seam side down, on top of the first ball.

17 Using your forefinger, press through the centre of the balls down to the baking sheet.

18 Repeat with the remaining 2 dough balls, to shape a second loaf.

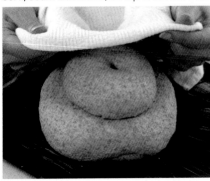

19 Cover both loaves with tea towels. Leave in a warm place for 45 minutes or until doubled.

20 Preheat the oven to 190°C (375°F/Gas 5). Bake for 40–45 minutes until well browned.

21 The loaves should sound hollow when tapped on the base. Cool on a wire rack.

Classic Loaf variations

White Loaf

Mastering a classic white loaf should be a rite of passage for all amateur bakers. Nothing beats the taste of fresh, crusty white bread, still warm from the oven.

| MAKES 1 LOAF | 20 MINS | 40–45 MINS | UP TO 4 WEEKS |

Rising and proving time
2–3 hrs

Ingredients
500g (1lb 2oz) very strong white bread flour, plus extra for dusting
1 tsp fine salt
2 tsp dried yeast
1 tbsp sunflower oil, plus extra for greasing

Method

1 Put the flour and salt into a bowl. In a small bowl, dissolve the dried yeast in 300ml (10fl oz) warm water. Once it has dissolved, add the oil. Make a well in the centre of the flour. Pour in the liquid, stirring to form a rough dough. Use your hands to bring the dough together.

2 Turn the dough out onto a lightly floured work surface. Knead for 10 minutes until smooth, glossy, and elastic. Put the dough in a lightly oiled bowl, cover loosely with cling film and leave to rise in a warm place for up to 2 hours, until doubled in size.

3 When the dough has risen, turn it out onto a floured surface and knock it back to its original size. Knead it and shape it into the desired shape; I prefer a long, curved oblong shape known as a bloomer. Place the dough on a baking tray, cover it with cling film and a tea towel, and leave it in a warm place until well risen and doubled. This could take 30 minutes–1 hour. The bread is ready to bake when it is tight and well risen, and a finger poked into the dough leaves a dent which springs back quickly.

4 Preheat the oven to 220°C (425°F/Gas 7). Place one oven shelf in the middle of the oven, and one below it, close to the bottom of the oven. Boil a kettle. Now slash the top of the loaf 2 or 3 times with a knife on the diagonal. This will allow the bread to continue to rise in the oven. Dust the top with flour and place it on the middle shelf.

Place a roasting pan on the bottom shelf of the oven and then quickly pour the boiling water into it and shut the door. This will allow steam to be created in the oven and help the bread to rise.

5 Bake the bread for 10 minutes, then reduce to 190°C (375°F/Gas 5) and bake it for 30–35 minutes until the crust is golden brown and the bottom sounds hollow when tapped. Reduce to 180°C (350°F/Gas 4) if it is starting to brown too quickly. Remove the bread from the oven and leave to cool on a wire rack.

STORE Best eaten the day it is made, the loaf will store, wrapped in paper, in an airtight container overnight.

BAKER'S TIP

Tempting as it may be to taste the loaf as soon as it comes out of the oven, try to leave the bread to cool for at least 30 minutes before cutting. This will vastly improve the taste and texture of the finished loaf.

Walnut and Rosemary Loaf

A perfect combination of flavours; the texture of the nuts is fabulous.

MAKES 2 LOAVES | 20 MINS | 30–40 MINS | UP TO 12 WEEKS

Proving time
2 hrs

Ingredients

3 tsp dried yeast
1 tsp granulated sugar
3 tbsp olive oil, plus 2 tsp extra for
   oiling and glazing
450g (1lb) strong white bread flour,
   plus extra for dusting
1 tsp salt
175g (6oz) walnuts, roughly chopped
3 tbsp finely chopped rosemary leaves

Method

1 Mix the yeast and sugar in a small bowl, then stir in 100ml (3½fl oz) lukewarm water. Leave for 10–15 minutes or until the mixture becomes creamy. Lightly oil a large bowl.

2 Put the flour a in bowl with a pinch of salt and the olive oil, then add the yeast mixture and 200ml (7fl oz) lukewarm water. Mix the ingredients until they come together to form a dough. Knead the dough on a floured surface for 15 minutes. Knead in the walnuts and rosemary, then put the dough in the oiled bowl. Cover with a tea towel. Leave in a warm place for 1½ hours until doubled.

3 Knock the air out of the dough and knead for a few more minutes. Halve it, and shape each half into a 15cm (6in) round loaf. Cover with a towel and leave for 30 minutes to rise. Preheat the oven to 230ºC (450ºF/Gas 8) and oil a large baking sheet.

4 When the dough has doubled, brush with oil and place on the baking sheet. Bake on the middle shelf for 30–40 minutes until the loaves sound hollow when tapped on the base. Cool on a wire rack.

STORE Will keep for 1 day, wrapped in paper.

CLASSIC LOAF VARIATIONS

Pane di patate

Bread made with mashed potato has a soft crust and moist centre. In this recipe, the dough is coated in butter and baked in a ring mould.

MAKES 1 LOAF | **50–55 MINS** | **40–45 MINS** | **UP TO 8 WEEKS**

Rising and proving time
1½–2¼ hrs

Special equipment
1.75-litre (3-pint) ring mould, or 25cm (10in) round cake tin and a 250ml (8fl oz) ramekin

Ingredients
250g (9oz) potatoes, peeled and cut into 2–3 pieces
2½ tsp dried yeast
125g (4½oz) unsalted butter, plus extra for greasing
1 large bunch of chives, snipped
2 tbsp sugar
2 tsp salt
425g (15oz) strong white bread flour, plus extra for dusting

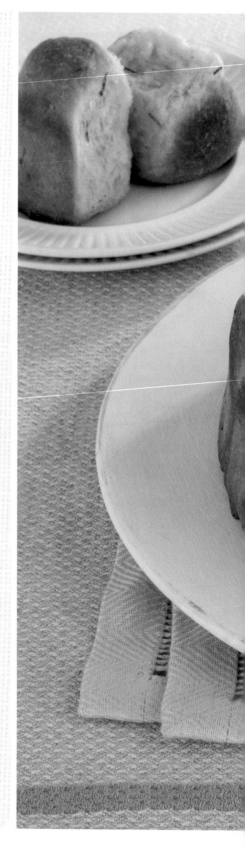

Method

1 Place the potatoes in a saucepan with plenty of cold water. Bring to a boil and simmer until tender. Drain, reserving 250ml (8fl oz) of the liquid. Mash with a potato masher. Let them cool.

2 In a small bowl, sprinkle the yeast over 4 tablespoons lukewarm water. Leave for 5 minutes until dissolved, stirring once. Melt half the butter in a pan. Put the reserved liquid, mashed potato, dissolved yeast, and melted butter into a bowl. Add the chives, sugar, and salt, and mix together thoroughly.

3 Stir in half the flour and mix well. Add the remaining flour, 60g (2oz) at a time, mixing well after each addition, until the dough pulls away from the sides of the bowl. It should be soft and slightly sticky. Knead the dough on a floured work surface for 5–7 minutes until smooth and elastic.

4 Grease a large, clean bowl. Put the dough in the bowl, and flip it so the surface is lightly buttered. Cover with a damp tea towel and let the dough rise in a warm place for 1–1½ hours until doubled in size.

5 Grease the ring mould or cake tin. If using a tin, grease the outside of the ramekin and place it upside down in the centre. Melt the remaining butter. Turn the dough out onto a lightly floured work surface and knock back. Cover and let rest for 5 minutes. Flour your hands and pinch off walnut-sized pieces of dough, making about 30 pieces. Roll each piece of dough into a smooth ball.

6 Put a few balls into the dish of melted butter and turn them with a spoon until coated. Transfer the balls of dough to the prepared mould or tin. Repeat with the remaining dough. Cover with a dry tea towel, and let the loaf rise in a warm place for 40 minutes until the mould or tin is full.

7 Preheat the oven to 190°C (375°F/Gas 5). Bake the bread for 40–45 minutes until it is golden brown and starts to shrink away from the mould. Let it cool slightly on a wire rack, then carefully unmould. With your fingers, pull the bread apart while still warm.

STORE This bread is delicious still warm from the oven, but can be tightly wrapped in paper and kept for 2–3 days.

PREPARE AHEAD The dough can be made, kneaded, and left to rise in the refrigerator overnight. Shape the dough, let it come to room temperature, then bake as directed.

BAKER'S TIP
This is both a classic Italian and an American recipe, where it is known as "monkey bread". It is designed to be placed in the centre of the dinner table and for diners to pull apart the sections with their fingers – great for a large family gathering.

CLASSIC BREADS

Dinner Rolls

You can shape the rolls however you like, though an assortment of different shapes looks very nice in a basket.

MAKES 16

45–55 MINS

15–18 MINS

8 WEEKS, UNBAKED

Rising and proving time
1½–2 hrs

Ingredients
150ml (5fl oz) milk
60g (2oz) unsalted butter, cubed,
  plus extra for greasing
2 tbsp sugar
3 tsp dried yeast
2 eggs, plus 1 yolk, for glazing
2 tsp salt

550g (1¼lb) strong white bread flour,
  plus extra for dusting
poppy seeds, for sprinkling (optional)

1 Bring the milk to a boil. Put 4 tablespoons into a small bowl and let cool to lukewarm.

2 Add the butter and sugar to the remaining milk in the pan until melted. Cool to lukewarm.

3 Sprinkle the yeast over the 4 tablespoons of milk. Leave for 5 minutes to dissolve. Stir once.

4 In a large bowl, lightly beat the eggs. Add the sweetened milk, salt, and dissolved yeast.

5 Gradually stir in the flour until the dough forms a ball. It should be soft and slightly sticky.

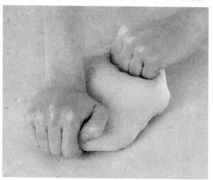

6 Knead the dough on a floured work surface for 5–7 minutes until very smooth and elastic.

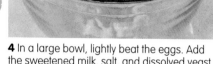

7 Put in an oiled bowl. Cover with cling film. Put in a warm place for 1–1½ hours until doubled.

8 Grease 2 baking sheets. Put the dough on a floured work surface and knock it back.

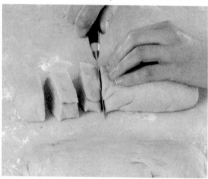

9 Cut in half, and roll each piece into a cylinder. Cut each cylinder into 8 equal pieces.

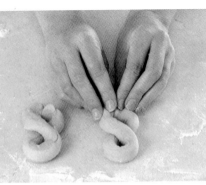

10 To shape round rolls, roll the dough in a circular motion so it forms a smooth ball.

11 For a baker's knot, roll into a rope, shape into an 8, and tuck the ends through the holes.

12 For a snail, roll into a long rope and wind it around in a spiral, tucking the end underneath.

13 Put on the baking sheets. Cover with a tea towel. Leave in a warm place for 30 minutes.

14 Preheat the oven to 220°C (425°F/Gas 7). Beat the egg yolk with a tablespoon of water.

15 Brush the rolls with the glaze and sprinkle evenly with poppy seeds (if using).

16 Bake for 15–18 minutes until golden brown. Serve warm. **PREPARE AHEAD** These rolls can be frozen at the shaping stage, brought back to room temperature, then glazed and baked.

Bread Roll variations

Spiced Cranberry and Pecan Rolls

These sweetened, fragrant rolls were adapted from a basic white bread recipe. Try adapting your own dough with different combinations of dried fruit, nuts, seeds, and spices.

MAKES 8 ROLLS | 20 MINS | 20–25 MINS | UP TO 4 WEEKS

Rising and proving time
2–3 hrs

Ingredients
500g (1lb 2oz) very strong white bread flour,
   plus extra for dusting
1 tsp fine salt
1 tsp mixed spice
2 tbsp caster sugar
2 tsp dried yeast
150ml (5fl oz) whole milk
50g (1¾oz) dried cranberries, roughly chopped
50g (1¾oz) pecans, roughly chopped
1 tbsp sunflower oil, plus extra for greasing
1 egg, beaten, for glazing

Method
1 Put the flour, salt, mixed spice, and sugar into a large bowl. Dissolve the yeast in 150ml (5fl oz) warm water. Once it has dissolved, add the milk and oil. Pour the liquid into the flour mixture, stirring it together to form a rough dough. Use your hands to bring the dough together.

2 Turn the dough out onto a lightly floured work surface. Knead the dough for 10 minutes, until it becomes smooth, glossy, and elastic.

3 Stretch the dough out thinly, scatter the cranberries and pecans over the surface and knead for 1–2 minutes more until the added ingredients are well incorporated. Put the dough in an oiled bowl, cover with cling film, and leave to rise in a warm place for up to 2 hours until doubled.

4 Turn the dough out onto a floured work surface and gently knock it back. Knead it briefly and divide it into 8 equal-sized pieces. Shape each into a plump, round roll. Try and poke any bits of fruit or nut that are sticking out back into the rolls, as these may burn on baking.

5 Place the rolls onto a large baking tray, cover loosely with cling film and a clean tea towel, and leave them to rise in a warm place for 1 hour until almost doubled in size. Preheat the oven to 200°C (400°F/Gas 6). Gently slash the top of the rolls in the shape of a cross with a sharp knife. This will allow the rolls to continue to rise in the oven. Lightly brush the tops with beaten egg and place them on the middle shelf of the oven.

6 Bake for 20–25 minutes until golden brown and the bottoms sound hollow when tapped. Remove the rolls from the oven and leave to cool on a wire rack.

STORE These are best eaten the day they are made, but will store, well wrapped in paper, in an airtight container overnight.

> **BAKER'S TIP**
> These are a delightful alternative to plain rolls, great for breakfast. Try making double quantity White Loaf dough (see page 20) and using half of it to make these rolls. They are especially welcome on Christmas morning, with the festive colours of the cranberries and warming fragrance of spices.

Sesame Seed Buns

These soft bread rolls are very easy to make and great for picnics or packed lunches, or for sandwiching home-made burgers at a summer barbecue.

MAKES 8 BUNS | 30 MINS | 20 MINS

Rising and proving time
1½ hrs

Ingredients
450g (1lb) strong white bread flour,
   plus extra for dusting
1 tsp salt
1 tsp dried yeast
1 tbsp vegetable oil, sunflower oil,
   or light olive oil, plus extra for greasing
1 egg, beaten
4 tbsp sesame seeds

Method
1 Stir the flour and salt together in a bowl, then make a well in the middle. Dissolve the yeast in 360ml (12fl oz) warm water, then add the oil. Tip this liquid into the well and quickly stir together. Leave for 10 minutes.

2 Turn the dough out onto a floured surface. Knead for 5 minutes or until smooth. Shape into a ball by bringing the edges into the middle, then turn into a oiled bowl, smooth side up. Cover with oiled cling film and leave in a warm place for 1 hour or until doubled.

3 Meanwhile, dust a baking tray with flour. Scoop the dough onto a floured surface, dust with a little flour, then knead briefly. Pull the dough into 8 even-sized pieces, then shape into rounds. Place onto the floured baking tray, well spaced apart, then leave for 30 minutes or until larger and pillowy. Preheat the oven to 200°C (400°F/Gas 6).

4 Once risen, brush the buns with egg and sprinkle sesame seeds over each. Bake for 20 minutes or until golden, risen, and round. Cool on a wire rack.

STORE These are best eaten the day they are made, but will store, well wrapped in paper, in an airtight container overnight.

Wholemeal Fennel Seed Rolls

Fennel seeds and cracked black pepper make these savoury rolls perfect for smoked ham sandwiches, or as buns for chorizo or pork burgers. Try experimenting with different whole spices, such as caraway or cumin.

MAKES 6 ROLLS	20 MINS	25–35 MINS	UP TO 12 WEEKS

Rising and proving time

2 hrs

Ingredients

2 tsp dried yeast
1 tsp demerara sugar
450g (1lb) plain wholemeal flour, plus extra for dusting
1½ tsp fine salt
2 tsp fennel seeds
1 tsp black peppercorns, cracked
olive oil, for greasing
1 tsp sesame seeds (optional)

Method

1 Sprinkle the yeast into a small bowl, add the sugar, and mix in 150ml (5fl oz) lukewarm water. Leave for about 15 minutes for the mixture to become creamy and frothy.

2 Mix the flour with a pinch of salt in a bowl, then add the yeast mixture, and gradually add a further 150ml (5fl oz) of lukewarm water. Mix until it comes together (it may need a little more water if it is too dry). Transfer to a lightly floured board and knead for about 10–15 minutes until smooth and elastic, then knead in the fennel seeds and cracked black pepper.

3 Lightly grease a bowl with olive oil. Sit the dough in the prepared bowl, cover with a tea towel, and leave somewhere warm for 1½ hours until doubled in size.

4 Knock back the dough and knead for a few more minutes, then divide into 6 pieces and shape each into a roll. Place them on an oiled baking sheet, cover, and leave to rise again for about 30 minutes. Preheat the oven to 200°C (400°F/Gas 6).

5 Brush the rolls with a little water, then sprinkle with sesame seeds (if using) and bake for about 25–35 minutes until the rolls are golden and sound hollow when tapped on the base. Allow to cool on the baking sheet for a few minutes, then transfer to a wire rack to cool completely.

STORE These are best eaten the day they are made, but will store, well wrapped in paper, in an airtight container overnight.

Pão de queijo

These unusual miniature cheese rolls, crisp on the outside and chewy on the inside, are a popular Brazilian street food.

MAKES 16	10 MINS	30 MINS	8 WEEKS, UNBAKED

Special equipment
food processor with blade attachment

Ingredients
125ml (4fl oz) milk
3–4 tbsp sunflower oil
1 tsp salt
250g (9oz) tapioca (manioc or cassava) flour, plus extra for dusting
2 eggs, beaten, plus extra for glazing
125g (4½oz) Parmesan cheese, grated

Method

1 Put the milk, sunflower oil, 125ml (4fl oz) water, and salt in a small saucepan and bring it to a boil. Put the flour into a large bowl and quickly mix in the hot liquid. The mixture will be very claggy and stuck together. Set aside to cool.

2 Preheat the oven to 190°C (375°F/Gas 5). Once the tapioca mixture has cooled, put it into a food processor. Add the eggs and process until all the lumps disappear, and it resembles a thick, smooth paste. Add the cheese and process together until the mixture is sticky and elastic.

3 Turn the mixture out onto a well-floured work surface and knead for 2–3 minutes until it is smooth and pliable. Divide the mixture into 16 equal pieces. Roll each piece into golf ball-sized balls and place, spaced apart, on a baking sheet lined with baking parchment.

4 Brush the balls with a little beaten egg and bake in the middle of the oven for 30 minutes, until well risen and golden brown. Remove them from the oven and let them cool for a few minutes before eating. These are best eaten the same day they are made, preferably still warm from the oven.

PREPARE AHEAD These can be open frozen on the baking sheet at the end of step 3 and transferred to freezer bags. Simply defrost for 30 minutes and bake as usual.

BAKER'S TIP

These classic Brazilian cheese rolls are made from tapioca flour (also known as manioc or cassava flour), and are thus wheat-free. The flour clumps when mixed with the liquid at first, but the use of a food processor will help enormously here. You will find that it soon becomes a smooth mass.

English Muffins

First popular in the 18th century, this traditional English teatime bread crossed the Atlantic to become an American breakfast staple.

MAKES 10 | 25–30 MINS | 13–16 MINS

Proving time
1½ hrs

Ingredients
1 tsp dried yeast
450g (1lb) strong white bread flour, plus extra for dusting
1 tsp salt
25g (scant 1oz) unsalted butter, melted, plus extra for greasing
vegetable oil, for greasing
25g (scant 1oz) ground rice or semolina

Method

1 Pour 300ml (10 fl oz) lukewarm water into a bowl, sprinkle over the yeast, and leave for 5 minutes to dissolve, stirring once. Mix the flour and salt in a large bowl. Make a well and pour in the yeast mixture and melted butter. Gradually draw in the flour to form a soft, pliable dough.

2 Knead the dough on a lightly floured surface for 5 minutes. Shape it into a ball and place in a large greased bowl. Cover with oiled cling film and leave in a warm place for 1 hour or until doubled in size.

3 Lay a tea towel on a tray, and scatter with most of the ground rice. Turn the dough out onto a floured surface, knead briefly, and divide it into 10 balls. Place the balls on the towel and press them into flattish rounds. Sprinkle with the rest of the ground rice, and cover with another tea towel. Leave to prove for 20–30 minutes until risen.

4 Heat a large, lidded frying pan and cook the muffins in batches. Cover with the lid and cook very gently for 10–12 minutes or until they puff up and the undersides are golden and toasted. Turn over and cook for 3–4 minutes or until golden underneath. Cool on a wire rack. Muffins are great split, toasted, and spread with butter and jam, or as the base for eggs Benedict.

> **BAKER'S TIP**
> Home-made muffins are far superior to anything you can buy, so it really is worth the extra effort of making them. Make the dough in the morning, and you can enjoy a freshly cooked batch for afternoon tea. Alternatively, leave to rise overnight, ready to bake for a leisurely breakfast.

Seeded Rye Bread

A crusty loaf accented by aromatic caraway seeds. Low-gluten rye is mixed with white flour to lighten it.

MAKES 1 LOAF | 35–40 MINS | 50–55 MINS | UP TO 8 WEEKS

Rising and proving time
2¼–2¾ hrs

Ingredients
2½ tsp dried yeast, dissolved in 4 tbsp lukewarm water
1 tbsp black treacle
1 tbsp caraway seeds
2 tsp salt
1 tbsp vegetable oil, plus extra for greasing
250ml (8fl oz) lager
250g (9oz) rye flour
175g (6oz) very strong white bread flour, plus extra for dusting
polenta (fine yellow cornmeal), for dusting
1 egg white, beaten until frothy, for glazing

1 Put the dissolved yeast, treacle, two-thirds of the caraway seeds, salt, and oil into a bowl.

2 Pour in the lager. Stir in the rye flour, and mix together well with your hands.

3 Gradually add the strong white flour until it forms a soft, slightly sticky dough.

4 Knead for 8–10 minutes until the dough is smooth and elastic, and put in an oiled bowl.

5 Cover with a damp tea towel. Leave in a warm place for 1½–2 hours until doubled.

6 Sprinkle a baking sheet with polenta. Knock back the dough on a floured work surface.

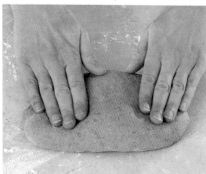

7 Cover and let it rest for 5 minutes. Pat the dough into an oval, about 25cm (10in) long.

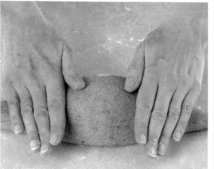

8 Roll it back and forth on the work surface, exerting pressure on the ends to taper them.

9 Transfer to the baking sheet. Cover and leave in a warm place for 45 minutes until doubled.

10 Preheat the oven to 190°C (375°F/Gas 5). Brush the beaten egg over the loaf to glaze.

11 Sprinkle with the remaining caraway seeds, and press them into the dough.

12 With a sharp knife, make 3 diagonal slashes, about 5mm (¼in) deep, on top.

13 Bake for 50–55 minutes until well browned. The bread should sound hollow when tapped on the base. Transfer to a wire rack and cool completely. **STORE** This loaf will keep, tightly wrapped in paper, for 2 days.

Rye Bread variations

Apricot and Pumpkin Seed Rolls

Rye flour is very dense, so mix it with white flour for a lighter texture.

| MAKES 8 ROLLS | 20 MINS | 30 MINS | UP TO 4 WEEKS |

Rising and proving time
up to 4 hrs

Ingredients
25g (scant 1oz) pumpkin seeds
2½ tsp dried yeast
1 tbsp black treacle
1 tbsp sunflower oil, plus extra for greasing
250g (9oz) rye flour
250g (9oz) very strong white bread flour, plus extra for dusting
1 tsp fine salt
50g (1¾oz) dried apricots, roughly chopped
1 egg, beaten, for glazing

Method

1 Toast the pumpkin seeds by dry-frying in a pan for 2–3 minutes, watching carefully to prevent them burning. Dissolve the dried yeast in 300ml (10fl oz) warm water. Add the treacle and oil and whisk to dissolve the treacle evenly. Put the 2 types of flour and the salt into a large bowl.

2 Pour the liquid into the flour mixture, stirring to form a rough dough. Turn the dough out on to a lightly floured work surface. Knead the dough for up to 10 minutes until smooth, glossy, and elastic.

3 Stretch the dough out thinly, scatter the apricots and pumpkin seeds over the surface, and knead for 1–2 minutes more until the added ingredients are well incorporated. Put into a oiled bowl, cover with cling film, and leave to rise in a warm place for up to 2 hours until well risen. This dough will not double in size as rye flour is very low in gluten, and rises slowly.

4 Turn it out on to a lightly floured work surface and gently knock it back. Knead it briefly and divide it into 8 equal-sized

pieces. Shape each into a plump, round roll. Try and poke any bits of fruit or seed that are sticking out back into the rolls, as these may burn on baking.

5 Place the rolls on a baking tray, cover with cling film and a tea towel, and leave them to prove in a warm place until well risen. This could take up to 2 hours. The rolls are ready to bake when they are tight and well risen, and a finger gently poked into the dough leaves a dent which springs back quickly.

6 Preheat the oven to 190°C (375°F/Gas 5). Brush the rolls with beaten egg and bake in the middle of the oven for 30 minutes until golden brown and the bottoms sound hollow when tapped. Remove the rolls from the oven and leave to cool on a wire rack.

STORE These are best eaten the same day, but will store overnight, well wrapped.

ALSO TRY...
Walnut Rye Bread Toast 75g (2½oz) walnuts by dry frying in a pan for 3–4 minutes. Rub in a clean tea towel to remove excess skin and roughly chop, then scatter the nuts over the thinly stretched dough, instead of the apricots and pumpkins. Once risen, shape into a single ball-shaped loaf by tucking the sides under the centre of the dough to get a tight, even shape, leaving the seam at the base; this is known as a boule. After it has risen a second time, bake for 45 minutes.

BAKER'S TIP
Here I have used apricot and pumpkin seeds, but dried cranberries, raisins, or blueberries would all work well too. As an alternative, you could also try other seeds, such as sesame or poppy seeds.

Pesto-filled Garland Bread

A loaf lightly flavoured with rye and spread with fragrant home-made pesto, this bread is perfect for serving at a buffet lunch or taking on a picnic, as the slices can be pulled off in individual portions. It also looks amazing!

MAKES 1 LOAF   **35–40 MINS**   **30–35 MINS**

Rising and proving time
1¾–2¼ hrs

Special equipment
food processor with blade attachment

Ingredients
2½ tsp dried yeast
125g (4½oz) rye flour
300g (10½oz) very strong white bread flour,
   plus extra for dusting
2 tsp salt
3 tbsp extra virgin olive oil,
   plus extra for greasing and glazing
leaves from 1 large bunch of basil
3 garlic cloves, peeled
30g (1oz) pine nuts, coarsely chopped
60g (2oz) freshly grated Parmesan cheese
freshly ground black pepper

Method

1 In a small bowl, sprinkle the yeast over 4 tablespoons taken from 300ml (10fl oz) lukewarm water. Let stand for about 5 minutes until dissolved, stirring once. Put the rye and white flour in a bowl along with the salt, and make a well. Combine the dissolved yeast and remaining water, pour into the well, and gradually draw in the flour. Mix well until it forms a soft, sticky dough.

2 Turn out the dough onto a floured surface and knead for 5 minutes until very smooth and elastic. Shape into a ball. Place in an oiled bowl. Cover with a damp tea towel and let rise in a warm place for 1–1½ hours until doubled in bulk.

3 Pulse the basil and garlic in the food processor. Work until coarsely chopped. With the blades turning, gradually add 3 tablespoons oil until smooth. Transfer the pesto to a bowl and stir in the pine nuts, Parmesan, and plenty of black pepper.

4 Brush a baking sheet with oil. Place the dough onto a floured surface and knead to knock out the air. Cover and let rest for about 5 minutes. Flatten the dough, then roll it into a 40 x 30cm (16 x 12in) rectangle with a rolling pin. Spread the pesto evenly over the dough, leaving a 1cm (½in) border. Starting with a long end, roll up the rectangle into an even cylinder. Running the length of the cylinder, pinch the seam firmly together. Do not seal the ends.

5 Transfer the cylinder, seam-side down, to the prepared baking sheet. Curve it into a ring, overlapping and sealing the ends. With a sharp knife, make a series of deep cuts around the ring, about 5cm (2in) apart. Pull the slices apart slightly, and twist them over to lie flat. Cover with a dry tea towel, and let rise in a warm place for about 45 minutes until doubled in bulk.

6 Preheat the oven to 220°C (425°F/Gas 7). Brush the loaf with oil and bake for 10 minutes. Reduce to 190°C (375°F/Gas 5), and bake for 20–25 minutes until golden. Cool slightly on a wire rack. Serve the same day.

Multi-grain Breakfast Bread

This hearty bread combines rolled oats, wheat bran, polenta, wholemeal and strong white flours, with sunflower seeds for added crunch.

MAKES 2 LOAVES	45–50 MINS	40–45 MINS	UP TO 8 WEEKS

Rising and proving time
2½–3 hrs

Ingredients
75g (2½oz) sunflower seeds
425ml (14½fl oz) buttermilk
2½ tsp dried yeast
45g (1½oz) rolled oats
45g (1½oz) wheat bran
75g (2½oz) polenta or fine yellow cornmeal, plus extra for dusting
45g (1½oz) soft brown sugar
1 tbsp salt
250g (9oz) strong wholemeal bread flour
250g (9oz) strong white bread flour, plus extra for dusting
unsalted butter, for greasing
1 egg white, beaten, for glazing

Method

1 Preheat the oven to 180°C (350°F/Gas 4). Spread the seeds on a baking sheet and toast in the oven until lightly browned. Let cool, then coarsely chop.

2 Pour the buttermilk into a saucepan and heat until just lukewarm. Sprinkle the yeast over 4 tablespoons lukewarm water. Set aside for 2 minutes, stir gently, then leave for 2–3 minutes until completely dissolved.

3 Put the sunflower seeds, rolled oats, wheat bran, polenta, brown sugar, and salt in a large bowl. Add the dissolved yeast and buttermilk, and mix together. Stir in the wholemeal flour with half the strong white flour, and mix well.

4 Add the remaining strong white flour, 60g (2oz) at a time, mixing well after each addition, until the dough pulls away from the sides of the bowl in a ball. It should be soft and slightly sticky. Turn the dough out onto a floured work surface and knead for 8–10 minutes until it is very smooth, elastic, and forms into a ball.

5 Grease a large bowl with butter. Put the dough in the bowl, and flip it so the surface is lightly buttered. Cover with a damp tea towel and leave to rise in a warm place for 1½–2 hours until doubled in size.

6 Sprinkle 2 baking sheets with polenta. Turn the dough out onto a lightly floured work surface and knock back. Cover, and let it rest for 5 minutes. With a sharp knife, cut the dough in half. Shape each half into a thin oval. Cover with a dry tea towel and leave to rise in a warm place for 1 hour or until doubled in size again.

7 Preheat the oven to 190°C (375°F/Gas 5). Brush the loaves with egg white, and bake for 40–45 minutes until the base of the loaves sound hollow when tapped. Transfer the loaves to a wire rack to cool completely.

STORE This bread is best on the day of baking, but can be tightly wrapped in paper and kept for 2–3 days.

BAKER'S TIP
Buttermilk is a great ingredient for bakers. Try adding it to any baking recipe that calls for milk. Its mild acidity brings a slight tang of sourness, while its active ingredients will lighten and soften the texture of many baked goods. You can find it in most supermarkets.

Anadama Cornbread

This dark, sweet cornbread originally hails from New England. It is curiously sweet and savoury at the same time, and keeps very well.

MAKES 1 LOAF	25 MINS	45–50 MINS	UP TO 8 WEEKS

Rising and proving time
4 hrs

Ingredients
125ml (4fl oz) milk
75g (2½oz) polenta or fine yellow cornmeal
50g (1¾oz) unsalted butter, softened
100g (3½oz) black treacle
2 tsp dried yeast
450g (1lb) plain flour, plus extra for dusting
1 tsp salt
vegetable oil, for greasing
1 egg, beaten, for glazing

Method

1 Heat the milk and 125ml (4fl oz) water in a small saucepan. Bring to a boil and add the cornmeal. Cook for 1–2 minutes or until it thickens, then remove from the heat. Add the butter and stir until it is well mixed. Beat in the treacle, then set aside to cool.

2 Dissolve the yeast in 100ml (3½fl oz) warm water and stir well. Put the flour and salt into a bowl and make a well. Gradually stir in the cornmeal mixture, then add the yeast mixture to make a soft, sticky dough.

3 Turn the dough out onto a lightly floured work surface. Knead for about 10 minutes until soft and elastic. It will remain fairly sticky, but should not stick to your hands. Knead in a little flour if it seems too wet. Put the dough in a lightly oiled bowl, cover loosely with cling film, and leave to rise in a warm place for up to 2 hours. The dough will not double in size, but should be very soft and pliable when well risen.

4 Turn the dough out onto a lightly floured work surface and gently knock it back. Knead it briefly and shape it into a flattened oval, tucking the sides underneath the centre of the dough to get a tight, even shape. Place on a large baking tray, and cover loosely with cling film and a clean tea towel. Leave it to rise in a warm place for about 2 hours. The dough is ready to bake when it is tight and well risen, and a finger gently poked into the dough leaves a dent that springs back quickly.

5 Preheat the oven to 180°C (350°F/Gas 4). Place one oven shelf in the middle of the oven, and one below it, close to the bottom. Boil a kettle of water. Brush the loaf with a little beaten egg, and slash the top 2–3 times with a sharp knife on the diagonal. Dust the top with a little flour, if desired, and place it on the middle shelf. Place a roasting pan on the bottom shelf, then quickly pour the boiling water into it and shut the door.

6 Bake for 45–50 minutes until the crust is nicely darkened and the bottom sounds hollow when tapped. Remove from the oven and leave to cool on a wire rack.

STORE The bread will keep, well wrapped in paper, in an airtight container for 5 days.

BAKER'S TIP
Slashing the loaf allows the bread to continue rising in the oven, as does the steam from the pan of boiling water, which also helps to give the bread a good crust. Anadama tastes wonderful with Emmental or Gruyère, or simply buttered and topped with some good ham and a little mustard.

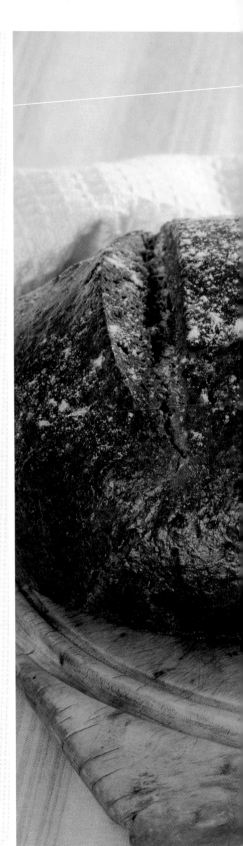

Ciabatta

One of the simplest breads to master, a good ciabatta should be well risen and crusty, with large air pockets.

| MAKES 2 LOAVES | 30 MINS | 30 MINS | UP TO 8 WEEKS |

Rising and proving time
3 hrs

Ingredients
2 tsp dried yeast
2 tbsp olive oil,
   plus extra for greasing
450g (1lb) strong white bread flour,
   plus extra for dusting
1 tsp sea salt

1 Dissolve the yeast in 350ml (11½fl oz) warm water, then add the oil.

2 Put the flour and salt in a bowl. Make a well, pour in the yeast, and stir to form a soft dough.

3 Knead on a floured surface for 10 minutes until smooth, soft, and somewhat slippery.

4 Put the dough in a lightly oiled bowl and cover loosely with cling film.

5 Leave to rise in a warm place for 2 hours until doubled. Turn out onto a floured surface.

6 Gently knock back the dough with your fists, then divide it into 2 equal pieces.

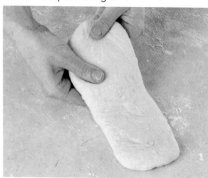

7 Knead them briefly and shape into traditional slipper shapes, around 30 x 10cm (12 x 4in).

8 Place each loaf on a lined baking sheet, with enough space around to allow it to expand.

9 Cover loosely with cling film and a tea towel. Leave for 1 more hour until doubled in size.

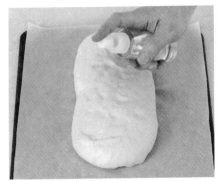

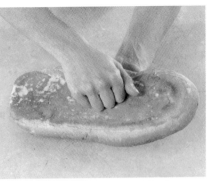

10 Preheat the oven to 230°C (450°F/Gas 8). Spray the loaves with a fine mist of water.

11 Bake on the middle shelf for 30 minutes, spraying them with water every 10 minutes.

12 It is cooked when the top is golden brown and the base sounds hollow when tapped.

13 When cooked, turn the loaves out onto a wire rack to cool for at least 30 minutes before cutting. **STORE** These are best eaten the same day, but can be stored overnight, wrapped in paper.

Ciabatta variations

Green Olive and Rosemary Ciabatta

Green olives and rosemary make a vibrant alternative to plain ciabatta.

MAKES 2 LOAVES · **40 MINS** · **30 MINS** · **UP TO 8 WEEKS**

Rising and proving time
3 hrs

Ingredients
1 quantity ciabatta dough,
  see page 40, steps 1–3
100g (3½oz) stoned green olives, drained,
  roughly chopped, and dried with kitchen paper
2 good sprigs of rosemary, leaves only,
  roughly chopped

Method

1 Once the dough has been kneaded for 10 minutes, stretch it out thinly on the work surface, scatter evenly with the olives and rosemary, and bring the sides together to cover the ingredients. Knead the dough until well incorporated. Put it in an oiled bowl, cover with cling film and leave to rise in a warm place for up to 2 hours until doubled.

2 Turn the dough out onto a floured work surface and knock it back. Divide it into 2 equal pieces. Knead the pieces and shape them into traditional slipper shapes, each 30 x 10cm (12 x 4in). Place each loaf on a lined baking sheet, with enough space around it to allow it to expand as it proves. Cover with cling film and a tea towel and leave for 1 hour until doubled in volume.

3 Preheat the oven to 230°C (450°F/Gas 8). Spray the loaves with a fine mist of water and bake in the centre of the oven for 30 minutes until golden brown; spray the loaves with water every 10 minutes. The bread is cooked when the underneath sounds hollow when tapped. Cool on a wire rack for 30 minutes before cutting.

STORE These are best eaten the same day. Can be stored overnight, loosely wrapped.

Ciabatta Crostini

Don't waste day-old ciabatta – slice it and bake the slices to make crostini, which will keep for days and can be used for snacks, canapés, or croutons. ▶

MAKES 25–30 · **15 MINS** · **10 MINS**

Ingredients
1 loaf day-old ciabatta bread,
  see pages 40–41
olive oil

For the toppings
100g (3½oz) rocket pesto, or
100g (3½oz) roasted red peppers, sliced
  and mixed with chopped basil, or
100g (3½oz) black olive tapenade topped
  with 100g (3½oz) goat's cheese

Method

1 Preheat the oven to 220°C (425°F/Gas 7). Slice the ciabatta into 1cm (½in) slices. Brush the tops with olive oil.

2 Bake them on the top shelf for 10 minutes, turning them after 5 minutes. Remove from the oven and cool on a wire rack.

3 Once cooled, top with any of the 3 suggested toppings, just before serving. If using the tapenade and goat's cheese topping, briefly grill before serving.

STORE The baked, unadorned crostini can be stored in an airtight container for 3 days. Add the topping just before serving.

Black Olive and Peppadew Ciabatta

Try using black olives and Peppadew peppers for a delicious ciabatta loaf studded with red and black. **PICTURED OVERLEAF**

MAKES 2 LOAVES · **40 MINS** · **30 MINS** · **UP TO 8 WEEKS**

Rising and proving time
3 hrs

Ingredients
1 quantity ciabatta dough,
  see page 40, steps 1–3
50g (1¾oz) stoned black olives, drained, roughly
  chopped, and dried with kitchen paper
50g (1¾oz) Peppadew red peppers, drained,
  roughly chopped, and dried with kitchen paper

Method

1 Once the dough has been kneaded for 10 minutes, stretch it out thinly on the work surface, scatter with the olives and peppers, and bring the sides together to cover the ingredients. Knead the dough briefly until they are incorporated. Put the dough in an oiled bowl, cover loosely with cling film and leave to rise in a warm place for up to 2 hours until doubled in size.

2 Turn the dough out onto a floured work surface and knock it back. Divide it into 2 pieces. Knead the pieces and shape them into 2 traditional slipper shapes, each 30 x 10cm (12 x 4in). Place each loaf on a lined baking sheet. Cover with cling film and a tea towel and leave for 1 hour until doubled.

3 Preheat the oven to 230°C (450°F/Gas 8). Spray the loaves with a mist of water and bake in the centre of the oven for 30 minutes until golden brown; spray the loaves with water every 10 minutes. The bread is cooked when the base sounds hollow when tapped. Cool for 30 minutes before cutting.

STORE Can be stored, wrapped, overnight.

BAKER'S TIP

Ciabatta dough should be wet and loose on kneading, as this will help to create the large air pockets traditionally found in the finished loaf. Wet doughs are easier to knead in a machine fitted with a dough hook, as they are a little sticky to manage well with your hands.

Rosemary Focaccia

A good-tempered dough that can be left in the refrigerator to rise overnight. Bring back to room temperature to bake.

SERVES 6–8 | 30–35 MINS | 15–20 MINS

Rising and proving time
1½–2¼ hrs

Special equipment
38 x 23cm (15 x 9in) Swiss roll tin

Ingredients
1 tbsp dried yeast
425g (15oz) strong white bread flour,
  plus extra for dusting
2 tsp salt
leaves from 5–7 rosemary sprigs,
  two-thirds finely chopped
90ml (3fl oz) olive oil,
  plus extra for greasing
¼ tsp freshly ground black pepper
sea salt flakes

1 Sprinkle the yeast over 4 tablespoons of warm water. Leave for 5 minutes, stirring once.

2 In a large bowl, mix the flour with the salt and make a well in the centre.

3 Add the rosemary, 4 tablespoons oil, yeast, pepper, and 240ml (8fl oz) lukewarm water.

4 Gradually draw in the flour and work it into the other ingredients to form a smooth dough.

5 The dough should be soft and sticky. Do not be tempted to add more flour to dry it out.

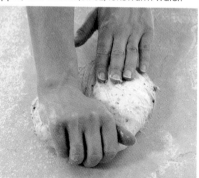

6 Sprinkle the dough with flour and knead for 5–7 minutes on a floured work surface.

7 When ready, the dough will be very smooth and elastic. Place in an oiled bowl.

8 Cover with a damp tea towel. Leave to rise in a warm place for 1–1½ hours until doubled.

9 Put the dough on a floured work surface and knock out the air.

10 Cover with a dry tea towel and let it rest for about 5 minutes. Brush the tin with oil.

11 Transfer the dough to the tin. With your hands, flatten the dough to fill the tin evenly.

12 Cover with a tea towel and leave to rise in a warm place for 35–45 minutes until puffed.

13 Preheat the oven to 200°C (400°F/Gas 6). Scatter the reserved rosemary leaves on top.

14 With your fingertips, poke the dough all over to make deep dimples.

15 Pour spoonfuls of the remaining oil all over the dough and sprinkle with the salt flakes.

16 Bake in the top shelf for 15–20 minutes until browned. Transfer to a wire rack. **ALSO TRY...**
Sage Focaccia Omit rosemary and black pepper at step 3. Add 3–5 sage sprigs, chopped.

Focaccia variations

Blackberry Focaccia

A sweet twist on a classic bread, perfect for a late summer picnic.

SERVES 6–8 | 30–35 MINS | 15–20 MINS

Rising and proving time
1½–2¼ hrs

Special equipment
38 x 23cm (15 x 9in) Swiss roll tin

Ingredients
1 tbsp dried yeast
425g (15oz) strong white bread flour,
 plus extra for dusting
1 tsp salt
3 tbsp caster sugar
90ml (3fl oz) extra virgin olive oil,
 plus extra for greasing
300g (10½oz) blackberries

Method

1 In a small bowl, sprinkle the yeast over 4 tablespoons lukewarm water. Let stand for 5 minutes until dissolved, stirring once.

2 In a large bowl, mix the flour with the salt and 2 tablespoons of the sugar. Make a well in the centre and add the dissolved yeast, 4 tablespoons of the oil, and 240ml (8fl oz) lukewarm water. Draw in the flour and mix to form a smooth dough. The dough should be soft and sticky; avoid adding more flour to dry it out.

3 Flour your hands and the dough, and turn it out onto a floured surface. Knead for 5–7 minutes until smooth and elastic. Transfer to an oiled bowl and cover with a damp tea towel. Leave to rise in a warm place for about 1–1½ hours until doubled in bulk.

4 Generously brush the tin with olive oil. Turn out the dough and knock out the air. Cover with a dry tea towel and leave to rest for 5 minutes. Transfer to the tin, flattening with your hands to fill the tin. Scatter the blackberries over the surface of the dough, cover, and leave to prove in a warm place for 35–45 minutes until puffed.

5 Preheat the oven to 200°C (400°F/Gas 6). Brush the dough with the remaining oil and sprinkle over the rest of the sugar. Bake at the top of the oven for 15–20 minutes until lightly browned. Cool slightly on a wire rack, then serve warm.

PREPARE AHEAD After kneading, at the end of step 3, the dough can be loosely covered with cling film and left to rise in the refrigerator overnight.

Fougasse

Fougasse is the French equivalent of the Italian focaccia, most associated with the region of Provence. The traditional leaf effect is surprisingly easy to achieve and looks lovely.

MAKES 3 LOAVES · **30–35 MINS** · **15 MINS**

Rising and proving time
6 hrs

Ingredients
5 tbsp extra virgin olive oil, plus extra for greasing
1 onion, finely chopped
2 back bacon rashers, finely chopped
400g (14oz) strong white bread flour,
  plus extra for dusting
1½ tsp dried yeast
1 tsp salt
sea salt flakes, for sprinkling

Method
1 Heat 1 tablespoon of the oil in a frying pan. Fry the onion and bacon until browned. Remove from the pan and set aside.

2 In a small bowl, add 150ml (5fl oz) warm water and sprinkle over the yeast. Leave to dissolve, stirring once. Place 200g (7oz) flour in a bowl, make a well in the middle, pour the yeast mixture into the well and draw in the flour to form a dough. Cover and leave to rise and then fall again, for about 4 hours.

3 Add the remaining flour, 150ml (5fl oz) water, salt, and the remaining oil, and mix well. Knead to a smooth dough on a lightly floured surface. Return to the bowl to rise for 1 hour or until doubled in size.

4 Line 3 baking sheets with parchment. Punch down the dough, then tip on the onion and bacon. Knead and divide the dough into 3 balls. Flatten each ball to 2.5cm (1in) high with a rolling pin, shape into a circle, and place on the baking sheets.

5 To create the leaf shapes, cut each circle with a sharp knife, twice down the centre, then 3 times on either side on a slant. Cut all the way through the thickness of the dough, but not through the edges. Brush with olive oil, sprinkle with sea salt, and leave to rise for 1 hour or until doubled.

6 Preheat the oven to 230°C (450°F/Gas 8). Bake for 15 minutes until golden. Remove from the oven and cool before serving.

Bagels

Making bagels is surprisingly simple. Try sprinkling with poppy or sesame seeds after brushing with egg.

MAKES 8–10	40 MINS	20–25 MINS	8 WEEKS, UNBAKED

Rising and proving time
1½–3 hrs

Ingredients
600g (1lb 5oz) strong white bread
 flour, plus extra for dusting
2 tsp fine salt
2 tsp caster sugar
2 tsp dried yeast
1 tbsp sunflower oil,
 plus extra for greasing
1 egg, beaten, for glazing

1 Put the flour, salt, and sugar in a bowl. Mix the yeast in 300ml (10fl oz) warm water.

2 Add the oil and pour the liquid into the flour mixture, stirring together to form a soft dough.

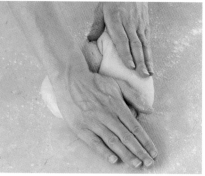

3 Knead on a floured surface for 10 minutes until smooth. Transfer to an oiled bowl.

4 Cover loosely with cling film and leave to rise in a warm place for 1–2 hours until doubled.

5 Transfer to a floured surface, push it back to its original size, and divide into 8–10 pieces.

6 Take each piece of dough and roll it under your palm to make a fat log shape.

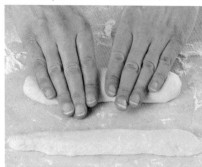

7 Using your palms, continue to roll it towards each end, until it is about 25cm (10in) long.

8 Take the dough and wrap it around your knuckles, so the join is underneath your palm.

9 Squeeze gently, then roll briefly to seal the join. The hole should still be big at this stage.

10 Transfer to 2 baking trays lined with baking parchment. Repeat to shape all the bagels.

11 Cover with cling film and a tea towel. Leave in a warm place for up to 1 hour until doubled.

12 Preheat the oven to 220°C (425°F/Gas 7), and set a large pan of water to boil.

13 Poach the bagels in gently simmering water for 1 minute on either side.

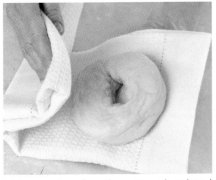

14 Remove them from the water with a slotted spoon. Dry them briefly on a clean tea towel.

15 Return the bagels to the baking trays and brush them with a little beaten egg.

16 Bake in the centre of the oven for 20–25 minutes until golden. Cool for 5 minutes on a wire rack before serving. **STORE** Best the day they are made, but still good toasted the next day.

Bagel variations

Cinnamon and Raisin Bagels

These sweet and spicy bagels are delicious fresh from the oven. Any leftovers can be trimmed of the crusts and turned into an alternative Bread and Butter Pudding (see page 168).

| MAKES 8–10 | 40 MINS | 20–25 MINS | 8 WEEKS, UNBAKED |

Rising and proving time
1½–3 hrs

Ingredients
600g (1lb 5oz) strong white bread flour, plus extra for dusting
2 tsp fine salt
2 tsp caster sugar
2 tsp ground cinnamon
2 tsp dried yeast
1 tbsp sunflower oil, plus extra for greasing
50g (1¾oz) raisins
1 egg, beaten, for glazing

Method
1 Put the flour, salt, sugar, and cinnamon into a large bowl. Dissolve the dried yeast in 300ml (10fl oz) warm water, whisking gently to help it dissolve, then add the oil. Gradually pour the liquid into the flour mixture, stirring to form a soft dough. Knead on a well-floured work surface, until smooth, soft, and pliable.

2 Stretch the dough out thinly, scatter the raisins evenly over it, and knead briefly until well mixed. Put it in an oiled bowl, cover with cling film and leave to rise in a warm place for 1–2 hours, until nearly doubled.

3 Place the dough on a floured surface and gently push it down until it is back to its original size. Divide it into 8–10 equal pieces. Take each piece and roll it under your palm to make a fat log shape. Using both your palms, continue to roll the dough outwards towards each end, until it is about 25cm (10in) long.

4 Wrap the dough round your knuckles, so the join is underneath your palm. Squeeze gently, then roll the bagel briefly to seal the join. The hole should still be quite big at this stage. Transfer to 2 baking trays lined with baking parchment and cover loosely with cling film and a tea towel. Leave in a warm place for up to 1 hour, until well puffed up and doubled in size.

5 Preheat the oven to 220°C (425°F/Gas 7) and set a large pan of water to boil. Gently poach the bagels, in batches of 3 or 4, in the simmering water for 1 minute, then flip them over and poach for another minute. Remove with a slotted spoon, dry briefly on a tea towel, then return to the baking trays. Brush with the beaten egg. Bake in the centre of the oven for 20–25 minutes until golden brown. Remove from the oven and cool for at least 5 minutes on a wire rack before eating.

STORE The bagels are best served the same day, but good toasted the next day.

Mini Bagels

Great for parties, try serving halved and topped simply with cream cheese, a curl of smoked salmon, lemon juice, and a sprinkling of cracked black pepper. ▶

| MAKES 16–20 | 45 MINS | 15–20 MINS | 8 WEEKS, UNBAKED |

Rising and proving time
1½–2½ hrs

Ingredients
1 quantity bagel dough, see page 50, steps 1–4

Method
1 When the dough has risen, place it on a floured work surface and gently knock it back. Divide it into 16–20 equal pieces, depending on the size of bagels you would like. Take each piece and roll it under your palm to make a log shape. Use both your palms to roll the dough outwards towards each end, until it is about 15cm (6in) long.

2 Take the dough and wrap it around the three middle fingers of your hand, so the join is underneath your palm. Pinch gently, then roll briefly to seal the join. The hole should still be quite big at this stage. Put the bagels on 2 baking trays lined with parchment, and cover loosely with cling film and a tea towel. Leave in a warm place for 30 minutes until well puffed up.

3 Preheat the oven to 220°C (425°F/Gas 7) and set a large pan of water to boil. Gently poach the bagels in batches of 6–8, poaching each side for just 30 seconds. Briefly dry the bagels with a tea towel, brush with the beaten egg, and bake for 15–20 minutes until golden brown. Remove from the oven and cool for at least 5 minutes on a wire rack before eating.

STORE These mini bagels are best served fresh the day they are made, but are also good toasted the next day.

BAKER'S TIP
The secret to cooking an authentic bagel is to poach the proven bagels briefly in simmering water before baking. It is this unusual step that helps to give them their classic chewy texture and soft crumb.

Pretzels

These German breads are great fun to make; the two-stage glazing method gives an authentic result.

MAKES 16 | 50 MINS | 20 MINS | UP TO 8 WEEKS

Rising and proving time
1½–2½ hrs

Ingredients
350g (12oz) strong white bread flour, plus extra for dusting
150g (5½oz) plain flour
1 tsp salt
2 tbsp caster sugar
2 tsp dried yeast
1 tbsp sunflower oil, plus extra for greasing

For the glaze
¼ tsp bicarbonate of soda
coarse sea salt or
2 tbsp sesame seeds
1 egg, beaten, for glazing

1 Put the 2 types of flour, salt, and sugar into a large bowl.

2 Sprinkle the yeast over 300ml (10fl oz) warm water. Stir, leave for 5 minutes, and add the oil.

3 Gradually pour the liquid into the flour mixture, stirring to form a soft dough.

4 Knead for 10 minutes until smooth, soft, and pliable. Transfer to an oiled bowl.

5 Cover loosely with cling film and leave in a warm place for 1–2 hours until nearly doubled.

6 Turn the dough out onto a lightly floured work surface, and gently knock it back.

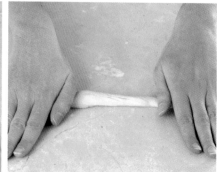

7 With a sharp knife, cut the dough neatly into 16 equal pieces.

8 Take each piece of dough and roll it under your palm to make a log shape.

9 Using your palms, continue to roll the dough towards each end, until it is 45cm (18in) long.

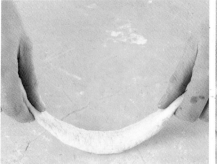

10 If difficult to stretch, hold by either end and rotate in a looping action, like a skipping rope.

11 Take each end of the dough and cross them over each other, forming a heart shape.

12 Now twist the ends around each other as though they had linked arms.

13 Secure the ends to the sides of the pretzel; it will appear quite loose at this stage.

14 Repeat to make 16 pretzels, placing them on baking sheets lined with parchment.

15 Cover with cling film and a tea towel. Leave in a warm place for 30 minutes until puffed up.

16 Preheat the oven to 200°C (400°F/Gas 6). Mix the soda in 2 tablespoons boiling water.

17 Brush the pretzels with the mixture. This gives them a dark colour and chewy exterior.

18 Scatter flakes of sea salt or sesame seeds over the brushed pretzels. Bake for 15 minutes.

19 Remove from the oven and brush with a little beaten egg. Bake for another 5 minutes.

20 Remove from the oven. The pretzels should be dark golden brown with a shiny finish.

21 Transfer to a wire rack and leave to cool for at least 5 minutes before serving.

Pretzel variations

Sweet Cinnamon Pretzels

A delicious sweet alternative to plain pretzels, these are definitely best eaten straight from the oven. Try toasting any leftover pretzels or gently reheating in a medium oven.

MAKES 16 **50 MINS** **20 MINS** **UP TO 8 WEEKS**

Rising and proving time
1½–2½ hrs

Ingredients
1 quantity unbaked pretzels,
  see pages 56–57, steps 1–15

For the glaze
¼ tsp bicarbonate of soda
1 egg, beaten
25g (scant 1oz) unsalted butter, melted
50g (1¾oz) caster sugar
2 tsp ground cinnamon

Method

1 Preheat the oven to 200°C (400°F/Gas 6). Dissolve the bicarbonate of soda in 2 tablespoons boiling water and brush it all over the shaped and risen pretzels. Bake for 15 minutes. Remove from the oven, brush all over with egg, and return to the oven for 5 minutes until dark golden brown and shiny.

2 Remove the pretzels from the oven and brush each one with melted butter. Mix the sugar and cinnamon on a plate and dip the buttered side of the pretzels into the mix. Leave to cool on a wire rack for at least 5 minutes before serving.

STORE These can be stored in an airtight container overnight.

BAKER'S TIP

Pretzels get their traditional mahogany colouring and chewy texture from a quick dip in bicarbonate of soda before cooking. The dough can be tricky to handle at home, so be sure to brush twice: first with bicarbonate of soda solution, and later with beaten egg, for an easy way to perfect pretzels.

Hot Dog Pretzels

These pretzeldogs are guaranteed to go down a storm at a children's party and are simple to prepare. They would make a great Bonfire Night treat, too. ➤

MAKES 8 **30 MINS** **15 MINS** **UP TO 8 WEEKS**

Rising and proving time
1½–2½ hrs

Ingredients
150g (5½oz) strong white bread flour,
  plus extra for dusting
100g (3½oz) plain flour
½ tsp salt
1 tbsp caster sugar
1 tsp dried yeast
½ tbsp sunflower oil, plus extra for greasing
8 hot dogs
mustard (optional)

For the glaze
1 tbsp bicarbonate of soda
coarse sea salt

Method

1 Put the two types of flour, salt, and sugar into a bowl. Sprinkle the yeast over 150ml (5fl oz) warm water. Stir once, then leave for 5 minutes until dissolved. Once it has dissolved, add the oil.

2 Pour the liquid into the flour mixture, stirring it together to form a soft dough. Knead for 10 minutes on a floured work surface until smooth, soft, and pliable. Put in a lightly oiled bowl, cover loosely with cling film, and leave in a warm place for 1–2 hours until nearly doubled in size.

3 Turn the dough out onto a floured work surface and knock it back. Divide it into 8 equal pieces. Take each piece of dough and roll it under your palm to make a log shape. Use both your palms to continue to roll the dough outwards towards each end, until it is about 45cm (18in) long. If the dough is difficult to stretch, hold it by either end and gently rotate it in a looping action as you would a skipping rope.

4 Take each hot dog and, if you like mustard (and don't mind the mess) brush with a little mustard. Starting at the top, wrap the pretzel dough around it in a circular twisting motion, so that the hot dog is completely sealed in, with only the top and the bottom showing. Pinch the dough together at the top and bottom to make sure it doesn't unwrap.

5 Place on baking sheets lined with baking parchment, cover with oiled cling film and a tea towel, and leave in a warm place for about 30 minutes until well puffed up. Preheat the oven to 200°C (400°F/Gas 6).

6 Dissolve the bicarbonate of soda in 1 litre (1¾ pints) boiling water in a pan. Poach the hotdogs, in batches of 3, in the simmering water for 1 minute. Remove with a slotted spatula, dry briefly on a tea towel, and return to the baking sheets.

7 Scatter with sea salt and bake for 15 minutes until golden brown and shiny. Remove from the oven and cool on a wire rack for 5 minutes before serving.

STORE These are best eaten while still warm, but can be stored in an airtight container in the refrigerator overnight.

artisan breads

Sourdough Loaf

A true sourdough starter uses naturally occurring yeasts to ferment. Dried yeast is a bit of a cheat, but more reliable.

MAKES 2 LOAVES | 45–50 MINS | 40–45 MINS | UP TO 8 WEEKS

Fermenting time
4–6 days

Rising and proving time
2–2½ hrs

Ingredients

For the starter
1 tbsp dried yeast
250g (9oz) strong white bread flour

For the sponge
250g (9oz) strong white bread flour,
   plus extra for sprinkling

For the bread
1½ tsp dried yeast
375g (13oz) strong white bread flour,
   plus extra for dusting
1 tbsp salt
vegetable oil, for greasing
polenta or fine yellow cornmeal,
   for dusting

1 Make the starter 3–5 days ahead. Dissolve the yeast in 500ml (16fl oz) lukewarm water.

2 Stir in the flour, and cover. Let it ferment in a warm place for 24 hours.

3 Look at the starter; it should have become frothy and have a distinct, sour odour.

4 Stir, cover, and ferment for 2–4 days longer, stirring it each day. Then use, or refrigerate.

5 For the sponge, mix 250ml (8fl oz) starter with 250ml (8fl oz) lukewarm water in a bowl.

6 Stir in the flour and mix vigorously. Sprinkle with 3 tablespoons flour.

7 Cover with a damp tea towel and leave it to ferment overnight in a warm place.

8 For the bread, dissolve the yeast in 4 tablespoons warm water. Mix into the sponge.

9 Stir in half the flour and the salt, and mix well to combine all the ingredients.

10 Gradually add the remaining flour. Mix well, until the dough forms a soft, slightly sticky ball.

11 Knead for 8–10 minutes until very smooth, and elastic. Put in an oiled bowl.

12 Cover with a damp tea towel and let rise in a warm place for 1–1½ hours until doubled.

13 Line two 20cm (8in) bowls with pieces of cloth, and sprinkle generously with flour.

14 Knock back the dough on a floured surface, cut in half, and shape each half into a ball.

15 Place in the bowls, covering with tea towels. Keep warm for 1 hour until the bowls are full.

16 Put a tin in the oven. Heat to 200°C (400°F/ Gas 6). Sprinkle 2 baking sheets with polenta.

17 Place the loaves, seam-side down, on the baking sheets and remove the cloth.

18 With a sharp knife, make criss-cross slashes on the top of each loaf.

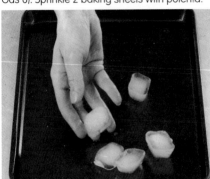

19 Put the loaves in the oven. Drop ice cubes into the roasting tin, then bake for 20 minutes.

20 Reduce to 190°C (375°F/Gas 5) and bake for another 20–25 minutes until well browned.

21 Transfer to a wire rack. **STORE** These can be kept for 2–3 days, tightly wrapped in paper.

Sourdough Bread variations

Sourdough Rolls

These pretty rolls are perfect
for a picnic lunch.

| MAKES 12 | 45–50 MINS | 25–30 MINS | UP TO 8 WEEKS |

Fermenting time
4–6 days

Rising and proving time
2–2½ hrs

Ingredients
1 quantity sourdough bread dough,
   see pages 62–63, steps 1–12

Method

1 Sprinkle 2 baking sheets with polenta.
Knock the air out of the dough and cut it in
half. Roll one piece into a cylinder 5cm (2in)
in diameter. Cut into 6 and repeat with the
remaining dough.

2 Lightly flour a work surface. Cup a piece
of dough under the palm of your hand and
roll to form a smooth ball. Repeat to shape
the remaining dough. Set the rolls on the
prepared baking sheets. Cover and let rise
in a warm place for about 30 minutes until
doubled in size.

3 Preheat the oven to 200°C (400°F/Gas 6).
Lightly sprinkle each roll with flour, then with
a sharp knife make criss-cross slashes in
the middle of each roll. Place a roasting tin
on the oven floor to heat up. Drop ice-cubes
into the roasting tin, then place the rolls in
the centre of the oven and bake for 25–30
minutes until golden and hollow-sounding
when tapped.

STORE The rolls will keep for 2–3 days,
tightly wrapped in paper.

PREPARE AHEAD These rolls can be frozen at
the shaping stage, brought back to room
temperature, then glazed and baked.

Fruit and Nut Sourdough Loaf

Raisins and walnuts are a great addition to a tangy sourdough loaf. Once you've learnt how to combine fruit and nuts into the dough, try experimenting with your own favourite combinations.

MAKES 2 LOAVES · 45–50 MINS · 40–45 MINS · UP TO 8 WEEKS

Fermenting time
4–6 days

Rising and proving time
2–2½ hrs

Ingredients
1 quantity starter and sponge,
  see page 62, steps 1–7

For the dough
2 tsp dried yeast
275g (10oz) strong white bread flour,
  plus extra for dusting
100g (3½oz) rye flour
1 tbsp salt
50g (1¾oz) raisins
50g (1¾oz) walnuts, chopped
vegetable oil, for greasing
polenta, for dusting

Method

1 Dissolve the yeast in 4 tablespoons lukewarm water. Leave for 5 minutes until frothy, then mix into the sponge. Combine the 2 types of flour and stir half the flour mix and all the salt into the sponge, mixing well. Add the remaining flour, mixing well, until the dough forms a soft, sticky ball.

2 Knead for 8–10 minutes on a floured surface, until smooth and elastic. Flatten the dough into a rough rectangle, scatter over the raisins and walnuts, and bring together, kneading in the fruit and nuts.

3 Place the dough in an oiled bowl, cover with a damp tea towel, and let rise in a warm place for 1–1½ hours until doubled in size. Line two 20cm (8in) bowls with pieces of cloth and sprinkle with flour. Knock back the dough on a floured surface, cut in half, and shape each half into a ball. Place in the bowls, cover with dry tea towels, and let rise in a warm place for 1 hour until the bowls are full.

4 Preheat the oven to 200°C (400°F/Gas 6) and heat a roasting tin on the oven floor. Sprinkle 2 baking sheets with polenta. Turn the loaves, seam-side down, onto the baking sheets. Make criss-cross slashes on the loaves using a sharp knife.

5 Drop ice cubes into the hot roasting tin, place the loaves in the oven, and bake for 20 minutes. Reduce to 190°C (375°F/Gas 5) and bake for another 20–25 minutes until well browned. Cool on a wire rack.

STORE The loaves will keep for 2–3 days, tightly wrapped in paper.

Pugliese

This classic Italian country loaf is flavoured and preserved with olive oil. Do not worry if the dough seems wet at first, as the looser the dough, the larger the air pockets in the finished crumb.

MAKES 1 LOAF · 30 MINS · 30–35 MINS · UP TO 4 WEEKS

Fermenting time
12 hrs or overnight

Rising and proving time
up to 4 hours

Ingredients

For the biga
¼ tsp dried yeast
100g (3½oz) strong white bread flour
olive oil, for greasing

For the dough
½ tsp dried yeast
1 tbsp olive oil, plus extra for greasing
300g (10½oz) strong white bread flour,
  plus extra for dusting
1 tsp salt

Method

1 For the biga, dissolve the yeast in 100ml (3½fl oz) warm water, whisking. Add the liquid to the flour and bring it together to form a dough. Place in an oiled bowl, cover with cling film and put in a cool place to rise for at least 12 hours, or overnight.

2 For the dough, dissolve the yeast in 140ml (4¾fl oz) warm water, then add the oil. Put the biga, flour, and salt into a bowl. Add the liquid. Stir it to form a rough dough. Knead for 10 minutes on a well-floured surface until smooth and elastic.

3 Put the dough in an oiled bowl, cover with cling film, and leave to rise in a warm place for up to 2 hours until doubled. Turn it out onto a floured surface. Knock it back and knead it into a shape; I like a rounded oblong.

4 Place the dough on a baking sheet, cover with oiled cling film and a tea towel, and leave in a warm place for up to 2 hours until doubled in size. The bread is ready to bake when it is tight and well risen, and a finger gently poked into the dough leaves a dent that springs back quickly. Preheat the oven to 220°C (425°F/Gas 7).

5 Slash the loaf in a slightly off centre line. Dust with flour, spray with water, and place on the middle shelf. Bake for 30–35 minutes. For a crisper crust, spray with water every 10 minutes. Remove from the oven and cool.

STORE The loaf will keep for 2–3 days, tightly wrapped in paper.

Baguette

Master this basic recipe and you can shape it to produce baguettes, ficelles, or bâtards whenever you like.

MAKES 2	30 MINS	15–30 MINS	UP TO 4 WEEKS

Fermenting time
12 hrs or overnight

Rising and proving time
3½ hrs

Ingredients

For the sponge
⅛ tsp dried yeast
75g (2½oz) strong white bread flour
1 tbsp rye flour
vegetable oil, for greasing

For the dough
1 tsp dried yeast
300g (10½oz) strong white bread
  flour, plus extra for dusting
½ tsp salt

1 Dissolve the yeast in 75ml (2½fl oz) warm water and add to the 2 types of flour.

2 Form a sticky, loose dough and place in an oiled bowl, with room for it to expand.

3 Cover with cling film and put in a cool place to rise for at least 12 hours.

4 To make the dough, dissolve the yeast in 150ml (5fl oz) warm water, whisking.

5 Put the risen sponge, flour, and salt into a large bowl and pour in the yeast liquid.

6 Stir it all together with a wooden spoon to form a soft dough.

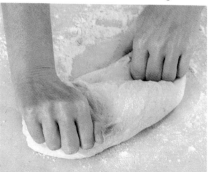

7 Knead for 10 minutes on a floured surface until smooth, soft, glossy, and elastic.

8 Place in an oiled bowl, cover with cling film, and leave to rise in a warm place for 2 hours.

9 Place it on a floured surface. Knock it back. Divide into 2 for baguettes or 3 for ficelles.

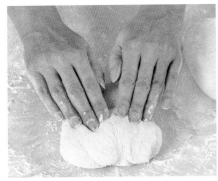

10 Knead briefly and shape each piece into a rectangle. Tuck one short edge into the centre.

11 Press down firmly, fold over the other short edge, and press firmly again.

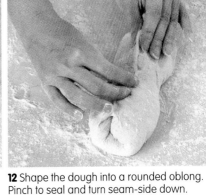

12 Shape the dough into a rounded oblong. Pinch to seal and turn seam-side down.

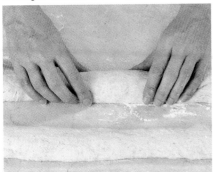

13 Shape into a long, thin log. A baguette is 4cm (1½in) wide, a ficelle 2–3cm (¾–1¼in).

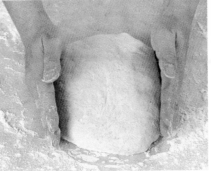

FOR A BÂTARD LOAF Knead all the dough briefly and shape it into a rough rectangle.

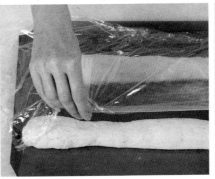

Tuck the furthest edge into the centre, press it, then do the same with the nearest edge.

Turn it over to tuck the seam underneath and gently shape it so it tapers at the ends.

14 Place the loaves on baking trays and cover with oiled cling film and a clean tea towel.

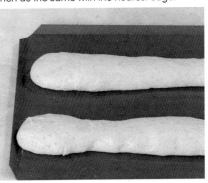

15 Keep warm for 1½ hours until doubled. Preheat the oven to 220°C (425°F/Gas 7).

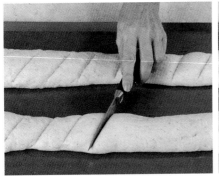

16 Slash the loaf deeply on the diagonal along the top, or criss-cross for a bâtard.

17 Dust with a little flour, spray it with water, and place on the middle shelf of the oven.

18 Bake for 15 minutes for a ficelle, 20 for a baguette, and 25–30 for a bâtard. Let it cool.

Baguette variations

Pain d'épi

This attractive variation on the baguette gets its name from its resemblance to wheat ears, "épi" in French. The wheat-ear effect is not too difficult to achieve and looks very decorative.

MAKES 3   40–45 MINS   25–30 MINS

Rising and proving time
4–5 hrs

Ingredients
2½ tsp dried yeast
500g (1lb 2oz) strong white bread flour,
   plus extra for dusting
2 tsp salt
unsalted butter, melted, for greasing

Method

1 Sprinkle the yeast over 4 tablespoons lukewarm water. Let it stand for 5 minutes until dissolved, stirring once.

2 Put the flour on a work surface with the salt. Make a well in the centre and add the dissolved yeast and 365ml (12fl oz) lukewarm water. Draw in the flour to form a dough. It should be soft and slightly sticky.

3 On a floured surface, knead the dough for 5–7 minutes until very smooth and elastic. Place the dough in a large bowl brushed with butter. Cover with a damp tea towel and leave to rise in a warm place for 2–2½ hours until tripled in size.

4 Turn the dough out onto a lightly floured work surface and knock back. Return to the bowl, cover, and leave to rise in a warm place for 1–1½ hours until doubled in size.

5 Sprinkle a cotton cloth with flour. Turn the dough onto a floured surface and knock back. Cut the dough into 3 equal pieces. Cover 2 pieces of dough while shaping the other. Flour your hands and pat the third piece into an 18 x 10cm (7 x 4in) rectangle.

6 Starting with a long side, roll the rectangle into a cylinder, pinching and sealing it with your fingers. Roll the cylinder, stretching it until it is a stick shape about 35cm (14in) long. Put the shaped loaf on the floured cloth. Repeat to shape the remaining dough, pleating the cloth between the pieces of dough.

7 Cover with a dry tea towel and let rise in a warm place for about 1 hour until doubled in size. Preheat the oven to 220°C (425°F/Gas 7). Set a roasting tin to heat on the floor of the oven. Sprinkle 2 baking sheets with flour. Roll 2 loaves onto 1 baking sheet, placing them 15cm (6in) apart. Roll the third loaf on to the other baking sheet.

8 Make a V-shaped cut about halfway through 1 of the loaves, 5–7cm (2–3in) from the end. Pull the point to the left. Make a second cut 5–7cm (2–3in) from the first, pulling the point to the right. Continue like this, shaping each loaf like "wheat ears". Drop ice cubes into the hot roasting tin and bake the loaves for 25–30 minutes until well browned and hollow-sounding when tapped. Leave to cool and eat the same day.

Wholemeal Baguette

Try this healthier, high-fibre alternative to a white baguette.

MAKES 2 | 20 MINS | 20–25 MINS | UP TO 4 WEEKS

Fermenting time
12 hrs or overnight

Rising and proving time
3½ hrs

Ingredients
1 quantity sponge, see page 68, steps 1–3,
 substituting wholemeal for the white bread flour

For the dough
½ tsp dried yeast
100g (3½oz) strong wholemeal bread flour
200g (7oz) strong white bread flour,
 plus extra for dusting
½ tsp salt

Method

1 To make the dough, dissolve the yeast in 150ml (5fl oz) warm water. Put the risen sponge, 2 types of flour, and salt into a large bowl. Gradually pour in the dissolved yeast, stirring together to form a dough.

2 Knead for 10 minutes on a floured work surface until smooth, glossy, and elastic. Put the dough in a lightly oiled bowl, cover loosely with cling film, and leave in a warm place for up to 1½ hours until doubled.

3 Turn the dough out onto a floured surface and knock it back. Divide into 2 equal pieces. Knead each piece and shape it into a rough rectangle. Use your hands to tuck the furthest edge of the dough into the centre, pressing it down with your fingertips, then do the same with the nearest edge. Fold the dough in half to make a long, thin oblong and press down to seal the edges.

4 Turn the dough over so the seam is underneath and use your hands to gently stretch and roll it into a long, thin log shape, no more than 4cm (1¾in) wide. Don't roll it longer than the length of a baking sheet, and bear in mind it will expand.

5 Place the loaves on 2 large baking sheets and cover loosely with oiled cling film and a tea towel. Leave in a warm place until well risen and almost doubled in size. This could take up to 2 hours. The bread is ready to bake when it is tight and well risen, and a finger gently poked into the dough leaves a dent that springs back quickly. Preheat the oven to 230°C (450°F/Gas 8).

6 Take a sharp knife and slash the top of the loaves deeply on the diagonal all along the top. This will allow the bread to continue to rise in the oven. Dust the tops with a little flour, if liked, spray with water, and place on the middle shelf of the oven. Bake for 20–25 minutes. For a crisper crust, spray the loaves with water every 10 minutes during baking. Remove the bread from the oven and cool on a wire rack.

STORE The baguettes can be stored, loosely wrapped in paper, overnight.

Artisan Rye Bread

Breads made with rye flour are very popular in central and eastern Europe. This version uses a starter.

MAKES 1 LOAF | 25 MINS | 40–50 MINS

Fermenting time
overnight

Rising and proving time
1½ hrs

Ingredients

For the starter
150g (5½oz) rye flour
150g pot live natural yogurt
1 tsp dried yeast
1 tbsp black treacle
1 tsp caraway seeds, lightly crushed

For the dough
150g (5½oz) rye flour
200g (7oz) strong white bread flour,
  plus extra for dusting
2 tsp salt
1 egg, beaten, for glazing
1 tsp caraway seeds, to decorate

1 In a bowl, mix all the starter ingredients together with 250ml (8fl oz) tepid water.

2 Cover and leave overnight. When you look at it the next day, it should be bubbling.

3 For the dough, mix the flours together with the salt, then stir into the starter.

4 Mix to make a dough, adding a little extra water if required.

5 Turn out onto a floured surface and knead for 5–10 minutes or until smooth and springy.

6 Shape into a ball, put into an oiled bowl, and cover loosely with cling film.

7 Leave in a warm place for 1 hour or until doubled in size.

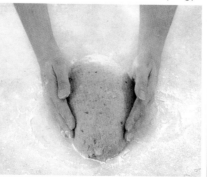

8 Flour a baking tray. Lightly knead the dough again, then form it into a rugby-ball shape.

9 Lift onto the tray, re-cover it loosely, and leave to rise again for another 30 minutes.

10 Preheat the oven to 220°C (425°F/Gas 7). Brush the dough with the egg.

11 Immediately sprinkle evenly with the caraway seeds; they should stick to the egg.

12 Slash the loaf along its length. Bake for 20 minutes, then reduce to 200°C (400°F/Gas 6).

13 Bake for 20–30 minutes until dark golden. Cool on a wire rack. **STORE** Keeps well, wrapped, for 2–3 days. **ALSO TRY... Seeded Rye Bread** Knead in 100g (3½oz) mixed seeds, such as pumpkin, sunflower, sesame, poppy seeds, and pine nuts, at the end of step 5.

Artisan Rye Bread variations

Hazelnut and Raisin Rye Bread

The hazelnuts and raisins in this version add a little sweetness and crunch to the bread. Try experimenting with different combinations of your own favourite nuts and dried fruit.

MAKES 1 LOAF | 25 MINS | 40–50 MINS | UP TO 8 WEEKS

Fermenting, rising, and proving time
overnight, plus 1½ hrs

Ingredients

For the starter
150g (5½oz) rye flour
150g pot live natural yogurt
1 tsp dried yeast
1 tbsp black treacle

For the dough
150g (5½oz) rye flour
200g (7oz) strong white bread flour, plus extra for dusting
2 tsp salt
50g (1¾oz) hazelnuts, toasted, and roughly chopped
50g (1¾oz) raisins
vegetable oil, for greasing
1 egg, beaten, for glazing

Method

1 In a bowl, mix all the starter ingredients together with 250ml (8fl oz) tepid water. Cover and leave overnight. When you look at it the next day, it should be bubbling.

2 For the dough, mix the flours together with the salt, then stir into the starter. Mix to make a dough, adding extra water if required. Turn out onto a floured surface and knead for 5–10 minutes or until smooth and springy.

3 Stretch out the dough to a rough rectangle, scatter the hazelnuts and raisins on top, fold it over, and knead gently to incorporate. Shape the dough into a ball and place in an oiled bowl, covered with cling film. Leave in a warm place for 1 hour, until doubled.

4 Flour a baking tray. Lightly knead the dough again, then form it into a rugby-ball shape. Lift onto the tray, cover loosely with cling film, and leave to rise again for another 30 minutes.

5 Preheat the oven to 220°C (425°F/Gas 7). Brush the loaf with egg and slash along its length. Bake for 20 minutes. Reduce to 200°C (400°F/Gas 6) and bake for 20–30 minutes until dark golden. Cool on a wire rack.

STORE This rye bread will keep, wrapped in paper, for 2–3 days.

BAKER'S TIP
Rye bread makes a healthy alternative to sandwich bread. It is denser in the crumb and makes a more substantial bite. The addition of a variety of seeds, nuts, and dried fruit add crunch, extra nutrition, and texture to the finished bread. It is especially delicious with salt beef and pickles, or with cheese.

Pumpernickel

The unlikely inclusion of cocoa and coffee powder add depth of flavour.

MAKES 1 LOAF | 20 MINS | 30–40 MINS | UP TO 8 WEEKS

Fermenting time
12 hrs or overnight

Rising and proving time
4½ hrs

Special equipment time
1-litre (1¾-pint) loaf tin

Ingredients

For the starter
½ tsp dried yeast
75g (2½oz) rye flour
30g (1oz) live natural yogurt

For the dough
½ tsp dried yeast
1 tsp coffee powder
1 tbsp sunflower oil, plus extra for greasing
130g (4½oz) strong wholemeal bread flour,
  plus extra for dusting
30g (1oz) rye flour
½ tbsp cocoa powder
1 tsp salt
½ tsp caraway seeds, lightly pounded

Method

1 To make the starter, dissolve the yeast in 100ml (3½fl oz) warm water. Put the rye flour, yogurt, and yeasted liquid in a large bowl and stir well to combine. Cover with cling film and keep in a cool place to rise for at least 12 hours, or overnight.

2 To make the dough, dissolve the yeast in 3–4 tablespoons warm water. Add the coffee powder and stir until dissolved, then add the oil. Mix the starter, flours, cocoa powder, salt, and caraway seeds in a large bowl. Add the liquid.

3 Stir the ingredients, and when it seems a little stiff, use your hands to bring the dough together. Knead for 10 minutes on a lightly floured work surface until smooth, glossy, and elastic.

4 Put the dough in a lightly oiled bowl, cover loosely with cling film, and leave to rise in a warm place for up to 2 hours

until doubled in size. Turn it out onto a lightly floured work surface and gently knock it back. Shape it into a ball again, return to the bowl, and cover. Leave for 1 hour while it rises again.

5 Turn it out onto a lightly floured work surface and knock it back again. Knead it briefly and shape it into an oblong shape. Put it into a lightly oiled loaf tin, cover loosely with oiled cling film and a clean tea towel, and leave it to prove in a warm place for another 1½ hours until almost

doubled in size. It is ready to bake when it is tight and well risen, and a finger gently poked into the dough leaves a dent that springs back quickly. Preheat the oven to 200°C (400°F/Gas 6).

6 Bake in the centre of the oven for 30–40 minutes until risen and with a dark brown crust. Leave to cool on a wire rack.

STORE This keeps well, wrapped in paper, for 3 days.

Pane siciliano

This rustic semolina bread from Sicily toasts particularly well and makes deliciously crunchy bruschetta.

| MAKES 1 LOAF | 20 MINS | 25–30 MINS | UP TO 4 WEEKS |

Fermenting time
12 hrs or overnight

Rising and proving time
2½ hrs

Ingredients

For the starter
¼ tsp dried yeast
100g (3½oz) fine semolina or semolina flour
vegetable oil, for greasing

For the dough
1 tsp dried yeast
400g (14oz) fine semolina or semolina flour, plus extra for dusting
1 tsp fine salt
1 tbsp sesame seeds
1 egg, beaten, for glazing

Method

1 To make the starter, dissolve the yeast in 100ml (3½fl oz) warm water. Add the liquid to the semolina, and bring together to form a rough, loose dough. Place the dough in a lightly oiled bowl, with plenty of room for it to expand. Then cover it with cling film, and keep it in a cool place to rise for at least 12 hours or overnight.

2 To make the dough, dissolve the yeast in 200ml (7fl oz) warm water. Put the risen starter, flour, and salt into a large bowl. Add the dissolved yeast to the mixture.

3 Stir the ingredients with a wooden spoon and, when it seems a little stiff, use your hands to bring the dough together. Knead for up to 10 minutes on a floured work surface, until smooth, glossy, and elastic.

4 Put the dough in a lightly oiled bowl, cover loosely with cling film and leave to rise in a warm place for up to 1½ hours, until doubled in size.

5 Turn the dough out onto a floured work surface and gently knock it back. Knead it briefly, and mould it into the desired shape; traditionally a tight boule shape (see page 34, Walnut Rye Bread, for how to shape a boule). Place it on a large baking tray, and cover it loosely with oiled cling film and a clean tea towel. Leave it to prove in a warm place for 1 hour until almost doubled in size. The bread is ready to bake when it is tight and well risen, and a finger gently poked into the dough leaves a dent, which springs back quickly.

6 Preheat the oven to 200°C (400°F/Gas 6). Brush the top of the bread with the beaten egg, and scatter the sesame seeds over it. Bake the bread in the centre of the oven for 25–30 minutes until well risen and golden brown. Remove from the oven and transfer to a wire rack to cool for at least 30 minutes before serving.

STORE The bread can be stored, loosely wrapped in paper, for 2 days.

BAKER'S TIP
This bread can be made using either fine semolina or semolina flour. Semolina is made from durum wheat, so this bread is not wheat-free, but the semolina does give a deliciously rustic texture, similar to that of polenta or cornmeal. It is good on the side with an oil-rich tomato salad.

Schiacciata di uva

This sweet Italian "squashed" bread is very similar to a sweetened focaccia, and can be served cold or while still warm.

MAKES 1 LOAF **25 MINS** **20–25 MINS**

Rising and proving time
3 hrs

Special equipment
20 x 30cm (8 x 12in) Swiss roll tin

Ingredients

For the dough
700g (1lb 9oz) strong white bread flour, plus extra for dusting
1 tsp fine salt
2 tbsp caster sugar
1½ tsp dried yeast
1 tbsp olive oil, plus extra for greasing

For the filling
500g (1lb 2oz) small red seedless grapes, washed
3 tbsp caster sugar
1 tbsp finely chopped rosemary (optional)

Method

1 Put the flour, salt, and sugar into a large bowl. Dissolve the yeast in 450ml (15fl oz) warm water, then add the oil.

2 Gradually pour the liquid into the flour mixture, stirring together to form a soft dough. Knead for 10 minutes on a floured work surface, until smooth, glossy, and elastic. This dough should remain soft.

3 Put the dough in a lightly oiled bowl and cover it loosely with cling film. Leave it to rise in a warm place for up to 2 hours until doubled in size. Turn the dough out onto a floured work surface and gently knock it back. Knead it briefly and divide it into 2 portions, with roughly one-third of the dough in one and two-thirds in the other. Lightly oil the Swiss roll tin.

4 Take the largest piece of dough and roll it out roughly to the size of the tin. Place it in the tin and stretch it out to fill the tin, using your fingers to mould it to the sides.

Scatter two-thirds of the grapes over the surface, and sprinkle with 2 tablespoons of the caster sugar.

5 Roll out the smaller piece of dough to fit on top of the grapes, stretching it with your hands if necessary. Scatter the remaining grapes, and the chopped rosemary (if using) on the surface. Place the dough on a large baking tray, and cover it loosely with lightly oiled cling film and a clean tea towel. Leave it to prove in a warm place for up to 1 hour until well risen and almost doubled in size. Preheat the oven to 200°C (400°F/Gas 6).

6 Scatter the remaining tablespoon of caster sugar on top of the risen dough. Bake for 20–25 minutes until well risen and golden brown. Remove from the oven and allow to cool for at least 10 minutes before serving.

STORE Best eaten the day it is made, but will store, well wrapped in paper, overnight.

BAKER'S TIP

This unusual Italian flat bread is traditionally served to celebrate the grape harvest in the Tuscany region of Italy. It is best eaten the day it is made, and more or less sugar can be added to taste. Great with cheese and, of course, with Italian red wines.

flat breads & crisp breads

Four Seasons Pizza

If you prepare the sauce the day before and leave the bread to rise overnight, these are very quick to assemble.

MAKES 4 PIZZAS | **40 MINS** | **40 MINS**

Rising time
1–1½ hrs

Ingredients
500g (1lb 2oz) strong white bread
flour, plus extra for dusting
½ tsp salt
3 tsp dried yeast
2 tbsp olive oil, plus extra for greasing

For the tomato sauce
25g (scant 1oz) unsalted butter
2 shallots, finely chopped
1 tbsp olive oil
1 bay leaf
3 garlic cloves, crushed
1kg (2¼lb) ripe plum tomatoes,
deseeded and chopped
2 tbsp tomato purée
1 tbsp caster sugar
sea salt and freshly ground pepper

For the toppings
175g (6oz) mozzarella, thinly sliced
115g (4oz) mushrooms, thinly sliced
2 tbsp extra virgin olive oil
2 roasted red peppers, thinly sliced
8 anchovy fillets, halved lengthways
115g (4oz) pepperoni, thinly sliced
2 tbsp capers
8 artichoke hearts, halved
12 black olives

1 Mix the flour and salt. Dissolve the yeast in 360ml (12fl oz) tepid water, in a separate bowl.

2 Add the oil to the yeast mix, then combine with the dry ingredients. Mix to form a dough.

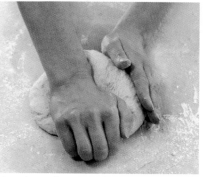

3 Knead on a floured surface for 10 minutes, or until the dough is smooth and elastic.

4 Roll the dough into a ball and place in an oiled bowl covered with oiled cling film.

5 Leave in a warm place for 1–1½ hours, until doubled; or store in the refrigerator overnight.

6 For the sauce, put a pan over low heat. Add the butter, shallots, oil, bay leaf, and garlic.

7 Stir, cover, and sweat the ingredients together for 5–6 minutes, stirring occasionally.

8 Add the tomatoes, tomato purée, and sugar. Cook for 5 minutes, stirring.

9 Now pour in 250ml (8fl oz) water, bring to a boil, and reduce the heat to a simmer.

10 Cook for 30 minutes, stirring, until reduced to a thick sauce. Season to taste.

11 Using a wooden spoon, press the sauce through a sieve. Cover and chill until needed.

12 To bake, preheat the oven to 200°C (400°F/Gas 6). Transfer the dough to a floured surface.

13 Knead lightly, divide into 4, and roll or press out into 23cm (9in) rounds.

14 Grease 4 baking sheets and carefully lift a pizza base onto each sheet.

15 Spread the sauce over the bases, leaving a 2cm (¾in) border around the edge of each.

16 Place any leftover sauce in a small freezer-safe container and freeze for later use.

17 Top the pizzas with mozzarella, dividing it equally between the bases.

18 Arrange the mushroom slices on a quarter of each pizza and brush with the olive oil.

19 Pile the roasted pepper slices on another quarter with the anchovy fillets on top.

20 Use pepperoni and capers for the third and artichokes and olives for the fourth quarter.

21 Bake at the top of the oven, 2 at a time, for 20 minutes or until golden brown. Serve hot.

Pizza variations

Pepper Calzone

"Calzone" means "trouser leg" in Italian, perhaps due to a resemblance or because this pizza turnover could be stuffed into a roomy trouser pocket!

MAKES 4 CALZONE | 25 MINS | 15–20 MINS

Rising and proving time
1½–2 hrs

Ingredients
1 quantity pizza dough, see pages 82–83, steps 1–5
4 tbsp extra virgin olive oil, plus extra to serve
2 onions, thinly sliced
2 red peppers, cored and cut into strips
1 green pepper, cored and cut into strips
1 yellow pepper, cored and cut into strips
3 garlic cloves, finely chopped
1 small bunch of any herb, such as rosemary, thyme, basil, or parsley, or a mixture, leaves finely chopped
sea salt
cayenne pepper, to taste
175g (6oz) mozzarella cheese, drained and sliced
plain flour, for dusting
1 egg, beaten, for glazing

Method
1 Heat 1 tablespoon oil in a pan, add the onions. Cook for 5 minutes until soft but not brown. Transfer to a bowl and set aside.

2 Add the remaining oil to the pan, followed by the peppers, garlic, and half the herbs. Season with salt and cayenne pepper. Sauté for 7–10 minutes, stirring, until soft but not brown. Add to the onions, and let cool.

3 Knock back the dough and divide into 4 equal pieces. Roll and pull each piece into a square about 1cm (½in) thick. Spoon the pepper mixture onto a diagonal half of each square, leaving a 2.5cm (1in) border.

4 Arrange the mozzarella on top. Moisten the edge of each square with water, and fold one corner over to meet the other, forming a triangle. Pinch the edges together. Put on a floured baking sheet. Let rise for 30 minutes. Preheat the oven to 230°C (450°F/Gas 8).

5 Whisk the egg with ½ teaspoon salt, and brush over. Bake for 15–20 minutes, until golden brown. Brush with a little olive oil before serving.

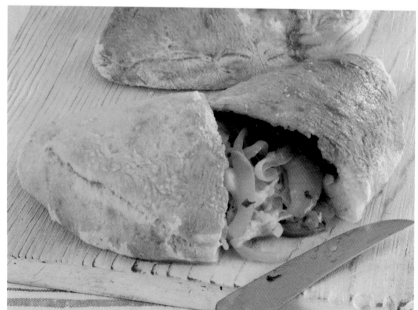

Chicago Deep-pan Pizza

A hearty pizza, dating back to 1940s Chicago.

SERVES 4 | 35–40 MINS | 20–25 MINS

Rising and proving time
1 hr 20 mins–1 hr 50 mins

Special equipment
2 x 23cm (9in) cake tins

Ingredients

For the dough
2½ tsp dried yeast
500g (1lb 2oz) strong white bread flour, plus extra for dusting
2 tsp salt
3 tbsp extra virgin olive oil, plus extra for greasing
2–3 tbsp polenta or cornmeal

For the sauce
375g (13oz) mild Italian sausage
1 tbsp olive oil
3 garlic cloves, finely chopped
2 x 400g cans chopped tomatoes
freshly ground black pepper
leaves from 7–10 flat-leaf parsley sprigs, chopped
175g (6oz) mozzarella cheese, torn into chunks

Method
1 In a small bowl, sprinkle the yeast over 4 tablespoons lukewarm water. Let it stand for 5 minutes, stirring once, until dissolved. In a large bowl, mix the flour with the salt and make a well in the centre. Add the dissolved yeast, 300ml (½ pint) lukewarm water, and the oil. Draw in the flour and work it into the other ingredients to form a smooth dough. It should be soft and slightly sticky.

2 Lightly flour a work surface, and knead the dough for 5–7 minutes until very smooth and elastic. Brush a large bowl with oil. Put the dough in the bowl and flip it so the surface is lightly oiled. Cover with a damp tea towel and let rise in a warm place for 1–1½ hours until doubled in size.

3 Slit the side of each sausage and push out the meat, discarding the casing. Heat the oil in a sauté pan. Add the sausage meat, and fry over medium-high heat, breaking up the meat with the wooden spoon, for 5–7 minutes until cooked. Reduce the heat to medium, remove the meat from the pan, and pour off all but 1 tablespoon of the fat.

4 Stir the garlic into the pan and fry for about 30 seconds. Return the sausage and stir in the tomatoes, salt, pepper, and all but 1 tablespoon of the parsley. Cook, stirring occasionally, for 10–15 minutes until thickened. Remove from the heat, taste for seasoning, and let cool completely.

5 Brush the tins with oil. Sprinkle the polenta into the tins, and turn it to coat the bottom and sides, then turn upside down and tap to remove the excess. Turn out the dough onto a lightly floured work surface and knock back. Shape the dough into 2 loose balls. With a rolling pin, roll the balls into rounds to fit your tins. Working carefully, wrap the dough around the rolling pin and drape it over each tin. With your hands, press the dough into the bottom of the tins, and 2.5cm (1in) up the sides, to form a rim. Cover with a dry tea towel and let rise for about 20 minutes. Preheat the oven to 230°C (450°F/Gas 8). Heat a baking sheet in the oven.

6 Spread the sauce over the dough, leaving a border. Sprinkle over the cheese and remaining parsley. Bake for 20–25 minutes until crisp and golden.

Pizza Bianca

This version is made without tomato sauce, kept moist with olive oil instead and packed with fresh Mediterranean flavours.

MAKES 4 PIZZAS | **25 MINS** | **20 MINS**

Rising time
1–1½ hrs

Ingredients
4 pizza bases, see pages 82–83,
 steps 1–5 and 12–14
4 tbsp extra virgin olive oil, plus extra for greasing
140g (5oz) Gorgonzola cheese, crumbled
12 slices Parma ham, torn into strips
4 fresh figs, each cut into 8 wedges, and peeled
2 tomatoes, deseeded and diced
115g (4oz) wild rocket leaves
freshly ground black pepper

Method
1 Preheat the oven to 200°C (400°F/Gas 6). Place the pizza bases on greased baking trays. Brush them with half the olive oil and scatter the cheese over the surface.

2 Bake in the oven for 20 minutes or until the bases are crisp and turning golden. Remove from the oven.

3 Arrange the ham, figs, and tomatoes on top. Then return to the oven for another 8 minutes or until the toppings are just warmed and the bases are golden brown.

4 Scatter over the rocket, season with plenty of black pepper, and serve at once, drizzled with the rest of the olive oil.

BAKER'S TIP
Pizzas are delicious with or without tomato sauce. However you like it, always remember that the toppings should be spread evenly over the base, and enough moisture added – either from tomato sauce, cheese, or extra virgin olive oil – to ensure the toppings remain well lubricated and appetizing.

Pissaladière

This French version of the Italian pizza derives its name from *pissala*, a paste made from anchovies.

SERVES 4 | 20 MINS | 1 HOUR 25 MINS | UP TO 12 WEEKS

Rising time
1 hr

Special equipment
32.5 x 23cm (13 x 9in) Swiss roll tin

Ingredients

For the base
225g (8oz) strong white bread flour, plus extra for dusting
sea salt and freshly ground black pepper

1 tsp soft brown sugar
1 tsp dried yeast
1 tbsp olive oil, plus extra for greasing

For the topping
4 tbsp olive oil
900g (2lb) onions, finely sliced
3 garlic cloves
sprig of thyme
1 tsp herbes de Provence (dry mix of thyme, basil, rosemary, and oregano)
1 bay leaf
100g jar anchovies in oil
12 black pitted niçoise olives, or Italian olives

Method

1 For the base, mix the flour, 1 teaspoon salt, and black pepper to taste in a large bowl. Pour 150ml (5fl oz) lukewarm water into a separate bowl, and use a fork to whisk in the sugar, then the yeast. Set aside for 10 minutes to froth, then pour into the flour with the olive oil.

2 Mix together to form a dough, adding 1–2 tablespoons lukewarm water if it looks too dry. Turn the dough out onto a lightly floured surface and knead for 10 minutes or until smooth and elastic. Shape it into a ball, put in a lightly oiled bowl, and cover with a tea towel. Leave in a warm place for 1 hour or until doubled in size.

3 For the topping, put the oil in a saucepan over very low heat. Add the onions, garlic, herbs, and bay leaf. Cover and sweat gently, stirring occasionally, for 1 hour or until the onions look like a purée. Be careful not to let the onions catch; if they begin to stick, add a little water. Drain well and set aside, discarding the bay leaf.

4 Preheat the oven to 180°C (350°F/Gas 4). Knead the dough briefly on a lightly floured surface, and roll it out so it is thin and large enough to fit in the Swiss roll tin. Press the dough into the tin and prick it with a fork.

5 Spread the onions over the base. Drain the anchovies, reserving 3 tablespoons oil, and slice the fillets in half lengthways. Embed the olives in rows in the dough and drape the fillets in a criss-cross pattern on top of the onions. Drizzle with the reserved anchovy oil and sprinkle with pepper.

6 Bake for 25 minutes or until the crust is brown. The onions should not brown or dry out. Remove and serve warm, cut into rectangles, squares, or wedges, or allow to cool before serving.

BAKER'S TIP
All the elements of pissaladière are very simple, so it is imperative that you use the best-quality ingredients for the finest result. Take care when selecting the anchovies, and make sure they are packed in good-quality oil. When you can find them, smoked anchovies make an amazing substitution.

Zweibelkuchen

The combination of sour cream and caraway seeds contrast well with the sweet, melting onions used to top this traditional German tart.

SERVES 8 | 30 MINS | 60–65 MINS

Rising and proving time
1½–2½ hrs

Special equipment
26 x 32cm (10 x 13in) baking tray with raised edges

Ingredients
4 tsp dried yeast
3 tbsp olive oil, plus extra for greasing
400g (14oz) strong white bread flour, plus extra for dusting
1 tsp salt

For the filling
50g (1¾oz) unsalted butter
2 tbsp olive oil
600g (1lb 5oz) onions, finely sliced
½ tsp caraway seeds
sea salt and freshly ground black pepper
150ml (5fl oz) soured cream
150ml (5fl oz) crème fraîche
3 eggs
1 tbsp plain flour
75g (2½oz) smoked streaky bacon, chopped

Method

1 To make the crust, dissolve the yeast in 225ml (7½fl oz) warm water. Add the olive oil and set aside. Sift the flour and salt into a large bowl. Make a well in the middle of the flour mixture and pour in the liquid ingredients, stirring all the time. Use your hands to bring the mixture together to form a soft dough. Turn it out onto a well-floured work surface and knead for 10 minutes until soft, smooth, and elastic.

2 Place the dough in a large, lightly oiled bowl, cover with cling film and leave to rise in a warm place for 1–2 hours until doubled in size.

3 To make the filling, heat the butter and olive oil in a large, heavy saucepan. Put in the onions and caraway seeds, and season well with salt and pepper. Cook gently for about 20 minutes, covered, until they are soft but not brown. Remove the lid and cook for another 5 minutes until any excess water evaporates.

4 In a separate bowl, whisk together the soured cream, crème fraîche, eggs, and plain flour, and season well. Mix in the cooked onions and set aside to cool.

5 When the dough has risen, turn it out onto a floured work surface and push it down gently with your knuckles to knock it back. Lightly oil the baking tray. Roll the dough out to roughly the size of the tray and line the tray with it, making sure the pie has an upturned edge. Use your fingers to ease the dough into position, if necessary. Cover with lightly oiled cling film and leave to rise in a warm place for another 30 minutes until puffy in places.

6 Preheat the oven to 200°C (400°F/Gas 6). Gently push down the dough if it has risen too much around the edges of the tray. Spread the filling out over the pie base, and sprinkle the chopped bacon on top.

7 Place the baking tray in the top shelf of the oven and bake for 35–40 minutes until golden brown. Remove from the oven and leave to cool for at least 5 minutes before serving. Serve warm or cold.

STORE Cover and chill overnight.

BAKER'S TIP

This delicious onion and sour cream tart looks like a cross between a pizza and a quiche, and is indeed made with a traditional pizza dough base. It is not much known outside its native Germany, but is well worth making. It was traditionally served during grape harvesting time.

Pita Bread

This pocket bread is delicious stuffed with salad and other fillings, or cut up and eaten with dips.

MAKES 6 | 20–30 MINS | 5 MINS | UP TO 8 WEEKS

Rising and proving time
1 hr–1 hr 50 mins

Ingredients
1 tsp dried yeast
60g (2oz) strong wholemeal
   bread flour
250g (9oz) strong white bread flour,
   plus extra for dusting
1 tsp salt
2 tsp cumin seeds
2 tsp olive oil, plus extra for greasing

1 In a bowl, mix the yeast with 4 tablespoons lukewarm water. Leave 5 minutes, then stir.

2 In a large bowl, mix together the 2 types of flour, salt, and cumin seeds.

3 Make a well and pour in the yeast, 190ml (6¾fl oz) lukewarm water, and oil.

4 Combine the flour mix with the wet ingredients, mixing to form a soft, sticky dough.

5 Turn the dough onto a floured work surface and knead until very smooth and elastic.

6 Place the dough in a lightly greased bowl and cover with a damp tea towel.

7 Leave to rise in a warm place for 1–1½ hours until doubled in size. Flour 2 baking sheets.

8 Turn the dough onto a lightly floured work surface, and knock back.

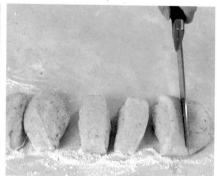

9 Shape the dough into a cylinder 5cm (2in) wide, then cut into 6 pieces.

10 Take 1 piece of dough and leave the rest covered with a tea towel as you work.

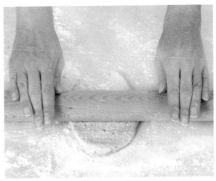

11 Shape the dough into a ball, then roll into an 18cm (7in) oval.

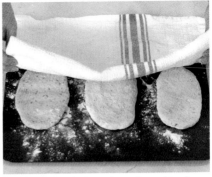

12 Transfer to a baking sheet. Repeat to shape the remaining pitas. Cover with a tea towel.

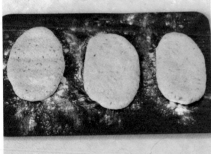

13 Leave in a warm place for 20 minutes and preheat the oven to 240°C (475°F/Gas 9).

14 Place another baking sheet in the oven. Once hot, transfer half the pitas to the sheet.

15 Bake for 5 minutes. Transfer to a wire rack and brush the tops lightly with water.

16 Bake the remaining rounds, transfer to the rack, and brush with water.
STORE Best eaten warm from the oven, pitas can be stored overnight in an airtight container.

Pita variations

Spiced Lamb Pies

Snacks such as these are found all around the Middle East.

MAKES 12 | 40–45 MINS | 10–15 MINS

Rising and proving time
1 hr–1 hr 50 mins

Ingredients
1 quantity pita dough, see pages 92, steps 1–8, omitting the cumin seeds
2 tbsp extra virgin olive oil
375g (13oz) lamb mince
sea salt and freshly ground black pepper
3 large garlic cloves, finely chopped
1cm (½in) piece of fresh root ginger, peeled and finely chopped
1 onion, finely chopped
½ tsp ground coriander
¼ tsp ground turmeric
¼ tsp ground cumin
large pinch of cayenne pepper
2 tomatoes, peeled, deseeded, and chopped
leaves from 5–7 coriander sprigs, finely chopped
Greek yogurt, to serve (optional)

Method

1 Heat the oil in a frying pan. Add the lamb, season, and stir over medium-high heat until evenly browned. Transfer to a bowl with a slotted spoon. Reduce the heat to medium, and pour off the fat, reserving 2 tablespoons. Add the garlic and ginger, and fry for 30 seconds. Put in the onion and stir until soft, then add the coriander, turmeric, cumin, cayenne pepper, lamb, and tomatoes. Cover and cook for 10 minutes until thickened.

2 Remove the pan from the heat. Stir in the chopped coriander leaves and taste for seasoning. Let the filling cool, then taste again: it should be well seasoned, so adjust if necessary.

3 Cut the dough in half. Shape 1 piece into a cylinder, 5cm (2in) in diameter. Cut into 6 pieces, and cover. Repeat to shape and divide the remaining dough. Shape 1 piece of dough into a ball. Roll out into a 10cm (4in) round. Spoon some lamb into the centre, leaving a 2.5cm (1in) border. Lift

the dough up and over the filling, to form a triangular parcel. Pinch the edges to seal. Place the pie on a baking sheet. Repeat to shape and fill the remaining dough.

4 Cover the pies with a tea towel and let rise in a warm place for 20 minutes. Preheat the oven to 230°C (450°F/Gas 8). Bake for 10–15 minutes, until golden brown. Serve warm, with Greek yogurt, if you like.

STORE The pies will keep in an airtight container overnight.

PREPARE AHEAD The lamb filling can be prepared, covered, and refrigerated 1 day ahead.

Spiced Chickpea Pitas

These are good chargrilled, and best eaten on the day they are made.

MAKES 8 | **25 MINS** | **15 MINS**

Rising time
1 hr

Ingredients
1 tsp dried yeast
1½ tsp cumin seeds, plus more for sprinkling
1½ tsp ground coriander
450g (1lb) strong white bread flour,
  plus extra for dusting
1 tsp salt
small bunch of coriander, roughly chopped
200g can chickpeas, drained and crushed
150g (5½oz) plain yogurt
1 tbsp extra virgin olive oil, plus extra for greasing

Method

1 Sprinkle the yeast over 300ml (10fl oz) lukewarm water and allow to dissolve, stirring once. Toast the cumin and ground coriander in a dry pan for 1 minute. Mix the flour and salt in a bowl. Stir in the spices, coriander, and chickpeas, then make a well in the middle. Pour in the yogurt, oil, and yeast liquid, and bring together to form a sticky dough. Set aside for 10 minutes.

2 Turn the dough out onto a floured surface, and knead it for 5 minutes, shaping it into a ball. Place the dough in an oiled bowl, cover it with oiled cling film, and leave it to rise in a warm place for 1 hour or until doubled.

3 Dust 2 baking trays with flour. Preheat the oven to 220°C (425°F/Gas 7). Turn the dough out onto a floured surface. Cut into 8 pieces.

4 Using a rolling pin, flatten them out into ovals, each about 5mm (¼in) thick. Place them on the baking trays, brush with oil, and scatter over cumin seeds. Bake for 15 minutes or until golden and puffed up.

STORE The pitas will keep in an airtight container overnight.

Pita Crisps

Serve these simple home-made pita crisps as part of a range of meze or starters for a healthier alternative to potato crisps.

SERVES 8 | **10 MINS** | **7–8 MINS**

Ingredients
6 pita breads, shop-bought,
  or see pages 92–93
extra virgin olive oil, for brushing
sea salt, for sprinkling
cayenne pepper, for sprinkling

Method

1 Preheat the oven to 230°C (450°F/Gas 8). Divide the pita breads in half, by separating the 2 layers of bread. Brush the bread on both sides with olive oil, then sprinkle them with salt and cayenne pepper.

2 Stack the bread pieces on top of each other in piles of 6, and cut them into large triangles. Lay the cut crisps on large baking sheets in a single layer, making sure they do not overlap.

3 Bake on the top shelf of the oven for 5 minutes or until the bottoms start to brown. Turn them over and cook for 2–3 minutes until they are browned and crisp. Leave to cool on kitchen paper before serving.

STORE The crisps will keep in an airtight container for 2 days.

BAKER'S TIP
These simple snacks go well with home-made dips and salsas, or even chilli con carne. They are an inexpensive alternative to crisps, and much healthier too! To make them even more nutritious, bake wholemeal pita crisps instead.

Naan Bread

This familiar Indian flat bread is traditionally cooked in a tandoor oven but this recipe uses a conventional oven.

MAKES 6 NAAN | 20 MINS | 8 MINS | UP TO 12 WEEKS

Rising time
1 hr

Ingredients

500g (1lb 2oz) strong white bread
  flour, plus extra for dusting
2 tsp dried yeast
1 tsp caster sugar
1 tsp salt
2 tsp black onion (nigella) seeds
100ml (3½fl oz) full-fat plain yogurt
50g (2oz) ghee, or butter, melted

1 Heat the ghee or butter in a small saucepan until melted. Set aside.

2 In a large bowl, mix together the flour, yeast, sugar, salt, and onion seeds.

3 Make a well. Add 200ml (7fl oz) lukewarm water, the yogurt, and the melted ghee.

4 Draw in the flour and mix gently with a wooden spoon to combine.

5 Keep mixing for 5 minutes until it forms a rough dough.

6 Cover and keep warm until doubled; about 1 hour. Preheat the oven to 240°C (475°F/Gas 9).

7 Place 2 baking trays in the oven. Knock back the dough.

8 Knead the dough on a floured surface until smooth. Divide into 4 equal pieces.

9 Roll each piece into an oval shape about 24cm (10in) long.

10 Transfer the bread to the preheated trays and bake for 6–7 minutes until well puffed.

11 Preheat the grill to its hottest setting. Transfer the bread to the grill pan.

12 Cook the naans for 30–40 seconds on each side or until they brown and blister.

13 When grilling, take care not to put the breads too close to the heat, to prevent burning. Transfer to a wire rack and serve warm.

ALSO TRY... Garlic and Coriander Naan Add 2 crushed garlic cloves and 4 tablespoons finely chopped coriander in step 2.

Naan variations

Feta, Chilli, and Herb-stuffed Naan

Try stuffing a simple naan bread dough with this herby feta mix for an unusual picnic dish, which brings together flavours of the Mediterranean with those of the Subcontinent.

MAKES 6 NAAN   **15 MINS**   **6–7 MINS**

Rising time
1 hr

Ingredients
500g (1lb 2oz) strong white bread flour, plus extra for dusting
2 tsp dried yeast
1 tsp caster sugar
1 tsp salt
2 tsp black onion (nigella) seeds
100ml (3½fl oz) full-fat plain yogurt
50g (2oz) ghee, or butter, melted
150g (5½oz) feta cheese, crumbled
1 tbsp finely chopped red chilli
3 tbsp chopped mint
3 tbsp chopped coriander

Method

1 In a bowl, mix together the flour, yeast, sugar, salt, and onion seeds. Make a well. Add 200ml (7fl oz) lukewarm water, the yogurt, and the ghee. Mix with a wooden spoon to combine. Mix for 5 minutes until it forms a smooth dough. Cover and keep warm for about 1 hour until doubled.

2 Make the stuffing by mixing together the feta, chilli, and herbs. Preheat the oven to 240°C (475°F/Gas 9) and place 2 large baking trays in the oven.

3 Divide the dough into 6 pieces, and roll each one out into a circle approximately 10cm (4in) in diameter. Divide the filling into 6 portions, and put a portion into the middle of each circle. Pull the edges up around the filling to form a purse shape. Pinch the edges to seal. Turn the dough over and roll out into an oval, taking care not to tear the dough.

4 Transfer the breads onto the preheated baking trays, and cook in the oven for 6–7 minutes or until well puffed. Transfer to a wire rack, and serve while still warm.

PREPARE AHEAD These can be stored overnight, wrapped in cling film. To reheat (from fresh or frozen), scrunch up a piece of greaseproof paper and soak it in water. Squeeze out the excess water and use to wrap the naan. Place them in a medium oven for 10 minutes until warm and soft.

Peshwari Naan

Children love these sweet, nutty stuffed naans, best eaten still warm from the pan, either as a dessert or a side dish to savoury curry. Try substituting finely chopped apple for the raisins and adding some cinnamon. ▶

MAKES 6 NAAN   **15 MINS**   **6–7 MINS**   **UP TO 8 WEEKS**

Rising time
1 hr

Special equipment
food processor with blade attachment

Ingredients
500g (1lb 2oz) strong white bread flour, plus extra for dusting
2 tsp dried yeast
1 tsp caster sugar
1 tsp salt
2 tsp black onion (nigella) seeds
100ml (3½fl oz) full-fat plain yogurt
50g (2oz) ghee, or butter, melted

For the stuffing
2 tbsp raisins
2 tbsp unsalted pistachios
2 tbsp almonds
2 tbsp dessicated coconut
1 tbsp caster sugar

Method

1 In a bowl, mix together the flour, yeast, sugar, salt, and onion seeds. Make a well. Add 200ml (7fl oz) lukewarm water, the yogurt, and the ghee. Mix with a wooden spoon to combine. Mix for 5 minutes until it forms a smooth dough. Cover and keep warm for about 1 hour until doubled.

2 Make the stuffing by whizzing together all the ingredients in a food processor, until finely chopped. Preheat the oven to 240°C (475°F/Gas 9) and place 2 baking trays in the oven.

3 Divide the dough into 6 pieces and roll each one out into a circle approximately 10cm (4in) in diameter. Divide the filling into 6 portions, and put a portion into the middle of each circle. Pull the edges up around the filling to form a purse shape. Pinch the edges together to seal.

4 Turn the dough over and roll out into an oval, taking care not to tear the dough or reveal any of the filling. Place on the preheated trays, and bake for 6–7 minutes or until well puffed. Transfer to a wire rack, and serve while still warm.

PREPARE AHEAD These can be stored overnight, wrapped in cling film. To reheat (from fresh or frozen), scrunch up a piece of greaseproof paper and soak it in water. Squeeze out the excess water and use to wrap the naan. Place them in a medium oven for 10 minutes until warm and soft.

BAKER'S TIP
Once you have mastered the art of stuffing and rolling out naan dough, there's no end to the number of things you can fill it with. Here the naan is stuffed with nuts, dried fruit, and coconut. Try a spiced lamb filling and serve with a minted yogurt dip.

Stuffed Paratha

These stuffed flat breads are quick and easy to make. Try doubling the quantities, then freezing half stacked between layers of greaseproof paper.

MAKES 4 | 20 MINS | 15–20 MINS | UP TO 8 WEEKS

Resting time
1 hr

Ingredients

For the dough
300g (10½ oz) chapatti flour
½ tsp fine salt
50g (1¾oz) unsalted butter,
  melted and cooled

For the stuffing
250g (9oz) sweet potato,
  peeled and diced
1 tbsp sunflower oil, plus
  extra for brushing
½ red onion, finely chopped
2 garlic cloves, crushed
1 tbsp finely chopped red chilli, or to taste
1 tbsp finely chopped fresh root ginger
2 heaped tbsp chopped coriander
½ tsp garam masala
sea salt

Method

1 To make the dough, sift the flour and salt together. Add the butter and 150ml (5fl oz) water, and bring the mixture together to form a soft dough. Knead for 5 minutes, then let the dough rest, covered, for 1 hour.

2 To make the stuffing, boil or steam the sweet potato for about 7 minutes until tender. Drain it well. In a frying pan, heat the oil over medium heat and fry the red onion for 3–5 minutes until soft but not golden. Add the garlic, chilli, and ginger, and continue to fry for 1–2 minutes.

3 Add the cooked onion mixture to the sweet potato, and mash well. You should not need extra liquid as the potato is quite moist and the oil from the onion mixture will help too. Add the coriander, garam masala, and a good seasoning of salt, and beat until smooth. Set aside to cool.

4 When the dough has rested, divide it into 4 pieces. Knead each piece and roll it out into a circle, around 10cm (4in) in diameter. Put a quarter of the stuffing in the middle. Pull the edges up around it, forming a purse shape.

5 Pinch the edges together to seal in the stuffing, turn the dough over, and roll it out into a circle, about 18cm (7in) in diameter, taking care not to roll too hard. If the filling bursts out, wipe it off and pinch the dough together to reseal the paratha.

6 Heat a large cast-iron frying pan or griddle (big enough to take the parathas) to medium heat. Fry the parathas for 2 minutes on each side, turning occasionally to make sure they are well cooked and browning in places. Once they have cooked on each side once, brush the surface with a little oil before turning them again. Serve immediately alongside a curry or as a light lunch dish with a green salad.

PREPARE AHEAD These can be stored overnight, wrapped in cling film. To reheat (from fresh or frozen), scrunch up a piece of greaseproof paper and soak it in water. Squeeze out the excess water and wrap in the paper. Place them in a medium oven for 10 minutes until warm and soft.

BAKER'S TIP

These Indian flat breads are made with traditional chapatti flour, but if you cannot find it easily, use plain wholemeal flour instead. Try stuffing them with a variety of fillings, including leftover vegetable curry, just make sure the ingredients are diced small so the stuffing is easily contained.

Tortillas

These classic Mexican flat breads are simple to make and far tastier than any shop-bought tortilla.

MAKES 8 | 10 MINS | 15–20 MINS | UP TO 8 WEEKS

Resting time
1 hr

Ingredients
300g (10oz) plain flour,
   plus extra for dusting
1 scant tsp salt
½ tsp baking powder
50g (1¾oz) lard or white vegetable
   fat, chilled and diced,
   plus extra for greasing

1 Put the flour, salt, and baking powder into a large bowl. Add the lard.

2 Rub the lard in with your hands until the mixture resembles fine crumbs.

3 Add 150ml (5fl oz) warm water. Bring the mixture together to form a rough, soft dough.

4 Turn it out onto a lightly floured work surface and knead for a few minutes until smooth.

5 Put the dough in a greased bowl and cover with cling film. Rest in a warm place for 1 hour.

6 Turn the dough out onto a floured work surface and divide it into 8 equal portions.

7 Take 1 piece and leave the others covered with cling film to prevent them from drying.

8 Roll each piece of dough out thinly to a circle about 20–25cm (8–10in) in diameter.

9 Stack the rolled tortillas in a pile. Place a piece of cling film or parchment between each.

10 Heat a frying pan over medium heat. Take a tortilla and dry fry for 1 minute.

11 Turn it over and continue to fry until both sides are cooked and browned in places.

12 Transfer to a wire rack and repeat to cook all the remaining tortillas. Serve warm or cool.

PREPARE AHEAD Cooled tortillas can be stored overnight, wrapped in cling film. To reheat from fresh or frozen, scrunch up greaseproof paper and soak it in water. Squeeze out the excess, use to wrap the tortillas, and bake in a medium oven for 10 minutes.

Tortilla variations

Quesadillas

Almost any filling works for quesadillas: try substituting chicken, ham, Gruyère cheese, or mushrooms.

MAKES 1 OF EACH | 5–10 MINS | 30–35 MINS

Ingredients

For the spiced beef and tomato filling
1 tbsp extra virgin olive oil
150g (5½oz) beef mince
pinch of cayenne pepper
sea salt and freshly ground black pepper
handful fresh flat-leaf parsley, finely chopped
2 tomatoes, diced
50g (1¾oz) Cheddar cheese, grated

For the avocado and spring onion filling
4 spring onions, finely chopped
1–2 fresh hot red chillies, deseeded and chopped
juice of ½ lime
½ avocado, peeled, stoned, and sliced
50g (1¾oz) Cheddar cheese, grated

For the tortillas
2 tbsp vegetable oil
4 tortillas, see pages 102–103

Method

1 For the beef filling, heat the oil in a pan. Fry the beef with the cayenne pepper on medium heat for 5 minutes or until no longer pink. Reduce the heat and loosen with a little hot water. Season, and cook for 10 minutes until the beef is cooked through. Stir in the parsley.

2 For the avocado filling, place the spring onions, chillies, and lime juice in a bowl. Season and mix. Set aside for 2 minutes.

3 Heat half the oil for the tortillas in a non-stick frying pan. Fry 1 tortilla for 1 minute or until lightly golden. Spoon the beef mixture over. Scatter over the tomato and cheese, then top with the other tortilla, pressing it down with the back of a fish slice to sandwich the two. Scoop the quesadilla up, carefully turn it over, and cook the other side for another minute or until golden. Slice in halves or quarters, and serve.

4 Heat the remaining oil in the frying pan, then fry 1 tortilla for 1 minute, or until golden. Scatter over the avocado, leaving a little space around the edge, and spoon on the spring onion mixture, and sprinkle with the cheese. Continue as in step 3.

Kids' Hot Tortilla Sandwiches

A quick alternative to a sandwich lunch that kids love.

SERVES 2 | 10 MINS | 8 MINS

Ingredients

4 tortillas, shop-bought, or see pages 102–103
4 thin slices of ham
ketchup, mild mustard, or chilli sauce (optional)
50g (1¾oz) grated cheese, such as Cheddar
carrots, peeled and chopped, to serve (optional)
cucumber, chopped, to serve (optional)

Method

1 Place 2 of the tortillas on the work surface. Place 2 slices of ham on each tortilla, trying to ensure that the ham covers the whole tortilla. Tear it a little and spread it out, if necessary.

2 Depending on your children's tastes, you could spread a little ketchup, mild mustard, or chilli sauce over the top of the ham. Sprinkle the grated cheese evenly over both the tortillas, and top with a second tortilla to make a sandwich.

3 Heat a large cast-iron frying pan or griddle (big enough to take the tortillas) to medium heat. Fry the tortillas one at a time for 1 minute on each side, until both sides are cooked and browned in places.

4 Cut each tortilla into 8 segments, as you would a pizza, and serve immediately, with some chopped carrot and cucumber for a quick lunch.

FLAT BREADS AND CRISP BREADS

Prawn and Guacamole Tortilla Stacks

These sophisticated Mexican-style canapés are simple to make.

MAKES 50 | **15 MINS** | **10–15 MINS**

Special equipment
3cm (1¼in) pastry cutter
piping bag with small plain nozzle

Ingredients
5 tortillas, shop-bought, or see pages 102–103
1 litre (1¾ pints) sunflower oil, for deep-frying
2 ripe avocados
juice of 1 lime
Tabasco sauce
4 tbsp finely chopped coriander
4 spring onions, trimmed and finely chopped
sea salt and freshly ground black pepper
25 cooked king prawns, peeled, deveined, and
 halved horizontally, or 50 prawns left whole

Method
1 Cut at least 100 disks out of the tortillas with the pastry cutter. Heat the oil in pan. Drop the tortillas into the oil, a handful at a time, and deep-fry until golden. Do not overcrowd the pan, or the tortillas will not crisp up properly. Remove them with a slotted spoon, and drain on kitchen paper. Cool.

2 In a bowl, mash the avocado with half the lime juice, dash of Tabasco, 3 tablespoons of the chopped coriander, chopped onions, and salt and pepper to taste.

3 When there are 30 minutes left before serving, marinate the prawns with the remaining lime juice and the rest of the chopped coriander.

4 Pipe a little guacamole on a tortilla, top it with another tortilla, pipe more guacamole on top, and finish with a curl of prawn. If the prawn is too big, twist it on the diagonal and stand it up in the guacamole.

PREPARE AHEAD The fried tortilla disks can be stored in an airtight container for 2 days.

Grissini

Tradition has it that breadsticks should be pulled the length of the baker's arm – these are more manageable!

MAKES 32

40–45 MINS

15–18 MINS

Rising time
1–1½ hrs

Ingredients
2½ tsp dried yeast
425g (15oz) strong white bread flour,
  plus extra for dusting
1 tbsp caster sugar
2 tsp salt
2 tbsp extra virgin olive oil
45g (1½oz) sesame seeds

1 Sprinkle the yeast over 4 tablespoons warm water. Leave for 5 minutes, stirring once.

2 Put the flour, sugar, and salt in a bowl. Add the yeast and 250ml (8fl oz) lukewarm water.

3 Add the oil and draw the flour into the liquid, mixing to form a soft, slightly sticky dough.

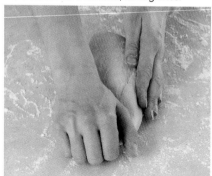

4 Knead the dough on a floured surface for 5–7 minutes until very smooth and elastic.

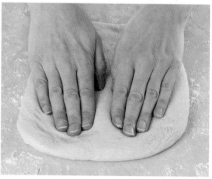

5 Cover the dough with a damp tea towel and let it rest for about 5 minutes.

6 Flour your hands and pat the dough into a rectangle on a well-floured work surface.

7 Roll the dough out to a 40 x 15cm (16 x 6in) rectangle. Cover it with a damp tea towel.

8 Leave in a warm place for 1–1½ hours until doubled. Preheat oven to 220°C (425°F/Gas 7).

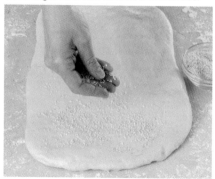

9 Dust 3 baking sheets with flour. Brush the dough with water. Sprinkle with sesame seeds.

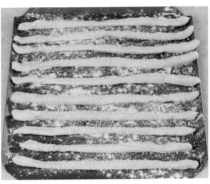

10 With a sharp knife, cut the dough into 32 strips, each about 1cm (½in) wide.

11 Stretch 1 strip to the width of a baking sheet. Set it on 1 of the baking sheets.

12 Repeat with the remaining strips, arranging them 2cm (¾in) apart.

13 Bake for 15–18 minutes until golden and crisp. Transfer to a wire rack and let cool completely.
STORE These will keep in an airtight container for 2 days.

Grissini variations

Spanish Picos

These miniature Spanish breadsticks are made by tying strips of dough in loops and are a great addition to a tapas meal.

MAKES 16 **40–45 MINS** **18–20 MINS**

Rising time
1–1½ hrs

Ingredients
½ quantity grissini dough, see page 106, steps 1–6
1½ tbsp sea salt

Method

1 Roll out the dough to a 20 x 15cm (8 x 6in) rectangle. Cover with a damp tea towel and leave to rise in a warm place for 1–1½ hours until doubled in size.

2 Preheat the oven to 220°C (425°F/Gas 7). Dust 2 baking sheets with flour. Cut the dough into 16 strips, then cut each strip into half. Take a half strip, loop it, and twist the ends in a single knot, and transfer to a prepared baking sheet. Shape the remaining strips in the same manner.

3 Lightly brush the loops with water and sprinkle with the sea salt. Bake the loops for 18–20 minutes until golden and crisp. Let cool as directed.

STORE The picos can be kept for 2 days in an airtight container.

Parmesan Grissini

Smoked paprika adds a depth of flavour to these cheesy grissini.

MAKES 32 **40–45 MINS** **10 MINS**

Rising time
1–1½ hrs

Ingredients
2½ tsp dried yeast
425g (15oz) strong white bread flour, plus extra for dusting
1 tbsp caster sugar
2 tsp salt
1½ tsp smoked paprika
2 tbsp extra virgin olive oil
50g (1¾oz) Parmesan cheese, grated

Method

1 Sprinkle the yeast over 4 tablespoons lukewarm water. Leave for 5 minutes until dissolved, stirring once. Put the flour, sugar, salt, and smoked paprika in a bowl. Pour in the oil, dissolved yeast, and 250ml (8fl oz) lukewarm water.

2 Draw in the flour to form a dough; it should be soft and sticky. Flour the surface and knead for 5–7 minutes until it is smooth and forms a ball. Cover with a damp tea towel and leave for 5 minutes. Flour your hands and pat the dough into a rectangle on a floured surface. Roll it out to a rectangle 40 x 15cm (16 x 6in). Cover with the tea towel, and leave for 1–1½ hours until doubled in size.

3 Preheat the oven to 220°C (425°F/Gas 7). Dust 3 baking sheets with flour and lightly brush the dough with water. Sprinkle with the Parmesan, pressing it down gently. With a sharp knife, cut the dough into 32 strips, each 1cm (½in) wide. Stretch 1 strip to the width of a baking sheet, and set on 1 of the prepared sheets. Repeat with the remaining strips, placing them 2cm (¾in) apart. Bake for 10 minutes until golden and crisp. Transfer to a wire rack to cool.

STORE These are best eaten fresh, but will keep in an airtight container for 2 days.

Parma Ham-wrapped Canapés

Try dipping these quick home-made canapés in herb mayo or salsa verde.

MAKES 32 **45 MINS** **15–18 MINS**

Rising time
1–1½ hrs

Ingredients
1 quantity grissini dough,
   see page 106, steps 1–8
3 tbsp sea salt
12 slices Parma ham

Method

1 Preheat the oven to 220°C (425°F/Gas 7) and dust 3 baking sheets with flour. Brush the rolled out dough with water and sprinkle with sea salt crystals.

2 With a sharp knife, cut the dough into 32 strips, each 1cm (½in) wide. Stretch each one to the width of the baking sheet and position 2cm (¾in) apart. Bake for 15–18 minutes until golden and crisp. Cool on a wire rack.

3 Cut each slice of Parma ham lengthways into 3. Wrap each grissini at one end with one-third of a slice of ham just before serving as a canapé.

PREPARE AHEAD The grissini can be made 1 day ahead and stored in an airtight container. Wrap with the Parma ham just before serving.

BAKER'S TIP
Home-made grissini are a lovely addition to a party menu. Experiment by adding flavour and texture, using items such as chopped olives, or smoked paprika, or your favourite cheeses; or leave them plain for a healthy and child-friendly snack. They will be at their best if eaten on the day they are baked.

Stilton and Walnut Biscuits

These savoury biscuits are an ideal way to use up the leftover Stilton and nuts you usually have after Christmas.

MAKES 24 | 10 MINS | 20 MINS | 12 WEEKS, UNBAKED

Chilling time
1 hr

Special equipment
5cm (2in) round pastry cutter

Ingredients
120g (4¼oz) Stilton cheese,
 or other blue cheese
50g (1¾oz) unsalted butter, softened
125g (4½oz) plain flour, sifted,
 plus extra for dusting
60g (2oz) walnuts, chopped
freshly ground black pepper
1 egg yolk

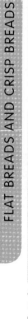

1 Mix together the cheese and butter in a bowl with an electric whisk until soft and creamy.

2 Add the flour to the cheese mixture and rub in with your fingertips to form breadcrumbs.

3 Add the walnuts and black pepper, and stir to mix through.

4 Finally add the egg yolk and bring the mixture together to form a stiff dough.

5 Knead the dough briefly on a lightly floured work surface to help blend in the walnuts.

6 Wrap the dough in cling film. Chill for 1 hour. Preheat the oven to 180°C (350°F/Gas 4).

7 Turn the dough out onto a floured work surface and knead briefly to soften slightly.

8 Roll it out to a thickness of 5mm (¼in) and cut out the biscuits with the pastry cutter.

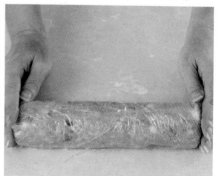

9 Alternatively, the dough can be chilled as an even 5cm (2in) diameter log.

10 Slice the dough log carefully into 5mm (¼in) rounds with a sharp knife.

11 Put the rounds on non-stick baking sheets and bake at the top of the oven for 15 minutes.

12 Turn them over and bake for another 5 minutes until golden brown on both sides.

13 Remove from the oven, allow to cool a little on their trays, then transfer to a wire rack to cool completely.
STORE The biscuits will keep in an airtight container for 5 days.

Cheese Biscuit variations

Parmesan and Rosemary Thins

These savoury biscuits are light and elegant, and are equally good served as an appetizer before a meal or after dinner with cheese.

MAKES 15–20 | 10 MINS | 15 MINS | 12 WEEKS, UNBAKED

Chilling time
1 hr

Special equipment
6cm (2½in) round pastry cutter
food processor with blade attachment (optional)

Ingredients
60g (2oz) unsalted butter, softened and diced
75g (2½oz) plain flour, plus extra for dusting
60g (2oz) Parmesan cheese, finely grated
freshly grated black pepper
1 tbsp chopped rosemary, or thyme, or basil

Method

1 Place the butter and flour in a bowl, or in the bowl of a food processor. Rub together with your fingertips, or pulse-blend, until the mixture resembles crumbs. Add the Parmesan, black pepper, and chopped herbs and mix in thoroughly. Bring the mixture together to form a dough.

2 Turn the dough out onto a floured surface and briefly knead to help it amalgamate. Wrap in cling film and chill for 1 hour.

3 Preheat the oven to 180°C (350°F/Gas 3). Turn the dough out onto a lightly floured surface and knead again to soften slightly.

4 Roll the dough out to 2mm (¹⁄₁₆in) thick and cut out biscuits with the pastry cutter. Place on several non-stick baking sheets and bake at the top of the oven for 10 minutes. Then turn them over and continue to bake for another 5 minutes until lightly browned.

5 Remove the biscuits from the oven and leave on the trays for 5 minutes, before transferring to a wire rack to cool completely.

STORE The thins will keep in an airtight container for 3 days.

Cheese Thins

These spicy biscuits can be made in bulk for an easy party snack.

MAKES 30 | 10 MINS | 15 MINS | 8 WEEKS, UNBAKED

Chilling time
1 hr

Special equipment
6cm (2½in) round pastry cutter
food processor with blade attachment (optional)

Ingredients
50g (1¾oz) unsalted butter, softened and diced
100g (3½oz) plain flour, plus extra for dusting
150g (5½oz) strong Cheddar cheese, finely grated
½ tsp smoked paprika or cayenne pepper
1 egg yolk

Method

1 Place the butter and flour in a bowl, or in the bowl of a food processor. Rub together with your fingertips, or pulse-blend, until the mixture resembles crumbs. Add the Cheddar and the paprika, and mix thoroughly. Add the egg yolk and bring the mixture together to form a dough.

2 Turn the dough out onto a floured surface and briefly knead to help it amalgamate. Wrap in cling film and chill for 1 hour. When ready to bake, preheat the oven to 180°C (350°F/Gas 4). Turn the dough out onto a lightly floured work surface and knead briefly again to soften slightly.

3 Roll the dough out to a thickness of 2mm (¹⁄₁₆in) and cut out the biscuits with the pastry cutter. Place the biscuits on several non-stick baking sheets and bake at the top of the oven for 10 minutes. Then turn them over, pressing them down gently with a spatula. Continue to bake for another 5 minutes until golden brown on both sides.

4 Remove the biscuits from the oven and leave them on the sheets for 5 minutes, before transferring to a wire rack to cool.

STORE The thins will keep in an airtight container for 3 days.

Cheese Straws

A great way of using up any leftover bits of hard cheese.

| MAKES 15–20 | 10 MINS | 15 MINS | 12 WEEKS, UNBAKED |

Chilling time
1 hr

Special equipment
food processor with blade attachment (optional)

Ingredients
75g (2½oz) plain flour, sifted,
 plus extra for dusting
pinch of salt
50g (1¾oz) unsalted butter, softened and diced
30g (1oz) strong Cheddar cheese, finely grated
1 egg yolk, plus 1 egg, beaten, for glazing
1 tsp Dijon mustard

Method
1 Place the flour, salt, and butter in a bowl, or the bowl of a food processor. Rub together with your fingertips, or pulse-blend, until the mixture resembles crumbs. Add the Cheddar and mix in. Whisk the egg yolk with 1 tablespoon cold water and the mustard until combined. Add to the crumbs and bring it together to form a dough.

2 Turn the dough out onto a lightly floured work surface and knead briefly. Wrap it in cling film and chill for 1 hour. Preheat the oven to 200°C (400°F/Gas 6). When ready to cook, briefly knead the dough again.

3 Roll the dough out to a 30 x 15cm (12 x 6in) rectangle; it should be 5mm (¼in) thick. With a sharp knife, cut 1cm (½in) wide strips along the shorter side. Brush the strips of pastry with a little beaten egg. Holding the top of each strip, twist the bottom a few times to form spirals.

4 Place the straws on non-stick baking sheets, pressing down the ends if the spirals appear to be unwinding. Bake at the top of the oven for 15 minutes. Cool on the trays for 5 minutes. Transfer to a wire rack to cool.

STORE The straws will keep in an airtight container for 3 days.

Oatcakes

These Scottish oatcakes are perfect with cheese and chutney. Made with just oatmeal (see Baker's Tip) they become a good wheat-free option.

| MAKES 16 | 20 MINS | 15 MINS | UP TO 4 WEEKS |

Special equipment
6cm (2½in) round pastry cutter

Ingredients
100g (3½oz) medium oatmeal,
  plus extra for dusting

100g (3½oz) wholemeal flour,
  plus extra for dusting
¾ tsp salt
freshly ground black pepper
½ tsp bicarbonate of soda
2 tbsp olive oil

Method

1 Preheat the oven to 180°C (350°F/Gas 4). Mix the dry ingredients together in a bowl. Whisk together the oil with 4 tablespoons of freshly boiled water. Make a well in the centre of the flour mixture and pour in the liquid. Mix together with a spoon to form a thick paste.

2 Lightly flour a work surface with a mixture of flour and medium oatmeal and turn the paste out onto it. Knead together briefly until it forms a dough. Gently roll the dough out to a thickness of 5mm (¼in); if you are making the dough with 100 per cent oatmeal (see Baker's Tip) it will be even more delicate and likely to crack.

3 Cut out as many oatcakes as possible, as it is difficult to bring the pastry together again after the first rolling. If the dough has difficulty coming together after the first cutting, put it back in the bowl and add a drop or two of water to help it amalgamate again, then re-roll and cut more oatcakes.

4 Place the oatcakes on several non-stick baking sheets and bake at the top of the oven for 10 minutes, then turn them over and continue to bake for another 5 minutes until golden brown on both sides. Remove the biscuits from the oven and leave on the trays for 5 minutes, before transferring to a wire rack to cool completely.

STORE The oatcakes will keep in an airtight container for 3 days.

BAKER'S TIP
These traditional Scottish biscuits can be made using just oatmeal, or with a mixture of both oatmeal and wholemeal flour. Made using only oatmeal, they are ideal for those who want to avoid wheat, but this will produce a more delicate, crumbly biscuit, and will need gentle handling when cutting.

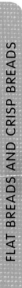

quick breads & batters

Soda Bread

This has a light, cake-like texture. As an added bonus, it requires no kneading, so is a wonderfully effort-free loaf.

MAKES 1 LOAF **10–15 MINS** **35–40 MINS**

Ingredients
unsalted butter, for greasing
500g (1lb 2oz) stone-ground
   strong wholemeal flour,
   plus extra for dusting
1½ tsp bicarbonate of soda
1½ tsp salt
500ml (16fl oz) buttermilk,
   plus extra if needed

1 Preheat the oven to 200°C (400°F/Gas 6). Grease a baking sheet with butter.

2 Sift the flour, bicarbonate of soda, and salt into a large bowl, tipping in any leftover bran.

3 Mix thoroughly to combine and make a well in the centre.

4 Gradually pour the buttermilk into the centre of the well.

5 With your hands, quickly draw in the flour to make a soft, slightly sticky dough.

6 Do not overwork the dough. Add a little more buttermilk if it seems dry.

7 Turn the dough out onto a floured surface, and quickly shape into a round loaf.

8 Put the loaf on the baking sheet and pat it down into a round, about 5cm (2in) high.

9 Make a cross 1cm (½in) deep in the top of the loaf with a very sharp knife or scalpel.

QUICK BREADS AND BATTERS

10 Bake the loaf in the preheated oven for 35–40 minutes, until brown.

11 Turn the loaf over and tap the bottom. The bread should sound hollow.

12 Transfer the bread to a wire rack and let it cool slightly.

13 Cut the bread into slices or wedges and serve warm. Soda bread also makes very good toast. **STORE** The bread will keep, well wrapped in paper, in an airtight container, for 2–3 days.

Soda Bread variations

Skillet Bread

In this version, the dough is cut in wedges and cooked in a heavy frying pan or skillet, and the addition of white flour makes it a little lighter.

MAKES 8 WEDGES   **5–10 MINS**   **30–40 MINS**

Special equipment
lidded cast-iron frying pan

Ingredients
375g (13oz) stone-ground strong wholemeal flour
125g (4½oz) strong white bread flour, plus extra for dusting
1½ tsp bicarbonate of soda
1 tsp salt
375ml (13fl oz) buttermilk
unsalted butter, melted, for greasing

Method
1 Put the 2 types of flour, the bicarbonate of soda, and salt into a large bowl. Make a well in the centre of the flour mixture, and pour the buttermilk into the well. Using your fingertips, quickly draw the flour into the liquid to make a soft dough. It should be slightly sticky.

2 Turn the dough out onto a lightly floured work surface and quickly shape it into a round loaf. Pat the dough with the palms of your hands to form a round shape, about 5cm (2in) high. With a sharp knife, cut the dough into 8 wedges.

3 Heat a large cast-iron frying pan to medium-low. Brush the heated pan with melted butter. In 2 batches, put the dough into the pan, cover, and cook, turning the wedges frequently, for 15–20 minutes, until golden brown and puffed. Serve warm.

Griddle Cakes

These sweet cakes are crisp on the outside, moist in the centre.

MAKES 20 CAKES   **5–10 MINS**   **10 MINS**

Special equipment
griddle or large cast-iron frying pan

Ingredients
250g (9oz) stone-ground strong wholemeal flour
1½ tsp bicarbonate of soda
1½ tsp salt
90g (3oz) rolled oats
3 tbsp soft brown sugar
600ml (1 pint) buttermilk
unsalted butter, melted, for greasing

Method
1 Put the flour, bicarbonate of soda, and salt into a large bowl. Stir in the oats and sugar, and make a well in the centre. Pour the buttermilk into the well. Stir, gradually drawing in the dry ingredients to make a smooth batter.

2 Heat a griddle or a large cast-iron frying pan, to medium-low. Brush the heated griddle with melted butter. Using a small ladle, drop about 2 tablespoons of the batter onto the hot surface. Repeat to make 5–6 cakes. Cook for about 5 minutes until the underside of the cakes are golden brown and crisp. Turn and brown them on the other side for about 5 minutes longer.

3 Transfer to a platter, cover, and keep warm. Continue with the remaining batter, brushing the griddle with more butter as needed. Serve the cakes warm.

American Soda Bread

This classic sweet bread can be ready for an afternoon snack in no time.

MAKES 1 LOAF	10–15 MINS	50–55 MINS	UP TO 8 WEEKS

Ingredients
400g (14oz) plain flour, plus extra for dusting
1 tsp fine salt
2 tsp baking powder
50g (1¾oz) caster sugar
1 tsp caraway seeds (optional)
50g (1¾oz) unsalted butter, chilled and diced
100g (3½oz) raisins
150ml (5fl oz) buttermilk
1 egg

Method

1 Preheat the oven to 180°C (350°F/Gas 4). In a large bowl, mix together the flour, salt, baking powder, caster sugar, and caraway seeds (if using). Rub in the butter until the mixture resembles fine crumbs. Add the raisins and mix well.

2 Whisk the buttermilk and the egg. Make a well in the centre of the flour mixture and pour in the buttermilk mixture, slowly stirring until it is all incorporated. You will need to use your hands at the end to bring the mixture together to form a loose, soft dough.

3 Turn the dough out onto a lightly floured surface and knead it briefly until smooth. Shape it into a round, about 15cm (6in) in diameter, and slash the top with a cross to allow the bread to rise easily when baking.

4 Place the dough on a baking tray lined with baking parchment and cook in the middle of the oven for 50–55 minutes until well risen and golden brown. Transfer to a wire rack and let it cool for at least 10 minutes before serving.

STORE This bread is best eaten the day it is made, but will keep, well wrapped in paper, for 2 days. It makes great toast.

Quick Pumpkin Bread

The use of grated pumpkin ensures this quick bread keeps moist for days. A perfect accompaniment for soup.

MAKES 1 LOAF	20 MINS	50 MINS	UP TO 8 WEEKS

Ingredients

300g (10½oz) plain flour, plus extra for dusting
100g (3½oz) wholemeal self-raising flour
1 tsp bicarbonate of soda
½ tsp fine salt

120g (4¼oz) pumpkin or butternut squash, peeled, deseeded, and roughly grated
30g (1oz) pumpkin seeds
300ml (10fl oz) buttermilk

1 Preheat the oven to 220°C (425°F/Gas 7). In a bowl, mix the flour, bicarbonate, and salt.

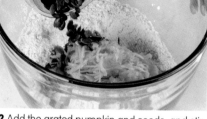

2 Add the grated pumpkin and seeds, and stir well to combine so that no clumps remain.

3 Make a well in the centre and pour in the buttermilk. Stir together to form a dough.

4 Use your hands to bring the mixture together into a ball, then turn out onto a floured surface.

5 Knead the dough for 2 minutes until it forms a smooth mass. You may need to add flour.

6 Shape the dough into a round 15cm (6in) in diameter. Place on a lined baking sheet.

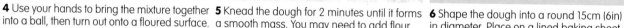

7 Use a sharp knife to slash a cross into the top. This helps the bread to rise when baking.

8 Cook for 30 minutes in the centre of the oven until risen. Reduce to 200°C (400°F/Gas 6).

9 Cook for a further 20 minutes. The base should sound hollow when tapped.

10 Transfer the bread to a wire rack and allow it to cool for at least 20 minutes before serving. **STORE** This will keep, well wrapped in paper, for 3 days. Cut the bread into wedges or slices and serve as an accompaniment to soups and stews.

Vegetable Quick Bread variations

Sweet Potato and Rosemary Rolls

The gentle scent of rosemary makes these rolls something special.

| MAKES 8 ROLLS | 20 MINS | 20–25 MINS | UP TO 8 WEEKS |

Ingredients

300g (10½oz) plain flour, plus extra for dusting
100g (3½oz) wholemeal self-raising flour
1 tsp bicarbonate of soda
½ tsp fine salt
freshly ground black pepper
140g (5oz) sweet potato, peeled and grated
1 tsp finely chopped rosemary
280ml (9fl oz) buttermilk

Method

1 Preheat the oven to 220°C (425°F/Gas 7). Line a baking sheet with parchment. In a bowl, mix the plain flour, wholemeal flour, bicarbonate of soda, salt, and pepper. Chop the grated potato to reduce the size of the shreds. Add it to the bowl, with the rosemary, mixing well.

2 Make a well in the centre of the dry ingredients and gently stir in the buttermilk, bringing the mixture together to form a loose dough. Use your hands to bring the mixture together into a ball, then turn it out onto a floured surface and knead for 2 minutes until it forms a smooth dough. You may need to add a little flour at this stage.

3 Divide the dough into 8 equal pieces, and shape them into tight rounds. Flatten the tops and cut a cross in the centre of each roll with a sharp knife to help the dough to rise in the oven.

4 Place the rolls onto the lined baking tray. Cook in the middle of the oven for 20–25 minutes until well risen and golden brown. Transfer to a wire rack and cool for at least 10 minutes before serving. These are particularly delicious eaten still warm.

STORE The rolls will keep, well wrapped in paper, for 3 days.

Courgette and Hazelnut Bread

Hazelnuts add taste and texture to this quick and easy bread.

| MAKES 1 LOAF | 20 MINS | 50 MINS | UP TO 8 WEEKS |

Ingredients

300g (10½oz) plain flour, plus extra for dusting
100g (3½oz) wholemeal self-raising flour
1 tsp bicarbonate of soda
½ tsp fine salt
50g (1¾oz) hazelnuts, roughly chopped
150g (5½oz) courgette, coarsely grated
280ml (9fl oz) buttermilk

Method

1 Preheat the oven to 220°C (425°F/Gas 7). Line a baking sheet with parchment. In a bowl, mix the plain flour, wholemeal flour, bicarbonate of soda, salt, and hazelnuts. Add the grated courgette, mixing it in well.

2 Make a well in the centre of the dry ingredients and stir in the buttermilk, bringing the mixture together to form a loose dough. Use your hands to bring the mixture together into a ball, then turn it out onto a floured surface and knead for 2 minutes until it forms a smooth dough. You may need to add a little extra flour at this stage.

3 Shape the dough into a round about 15cm (6in) in diameter. With a sharp knife, slash a cross in the top of the dough to help it to rise easily when baking.

4 Place the dough onto the baking sheet and cook in the middle of the oven for 30 minutes. Reduce to 200°C (400°F/Gas 6), and bake for 20 minutes until well risen, golden brown, and a skewer inserted into the middle emerges clean. Transfer to a wire rack and allow it to cool for at least 20 minutes before serving.

STORE The bread will keep, well wrapped in paper, for 3 days.

Parsnip and Parmesan Bread

A perfect combination of flavours to serve with a bowl of warming soup on a cold winter's day.

| MAKES 1 LOAF | 20 MINS | 50 MINS | UP TO 8 WEEKS |

Ingredients

300g (10oz) plain flour, plus extra for dusting
100g (3½oz) wholemeal self-raising flour
1 tsp bicarbonate of soda
½ tsp fine salt
freshly ground black pepper
50g (1¾oz) Parmesan cheese, finely grated
150g (5½oz) parsnip, coarsely grated
300ml (10fl oz) buttermilk

Method

1 Preheat the oven to 220°C (425°F/Gas 7). Line a baking sheet with parchment. In a bowl mix the plain flour, wholemeal flour, bicarbonate of soda, salt, pepper, and Parmesan. Roughly chop the grated parsnip to reduce the size of the shreds. Add it to the bowl, mixing it in well.

2 Make a well in the centre of the dry ingredients and gently stir in the buttermilk, bringing the mixture together to form a loose dough. Use your hands to bring the mixture together into a ball, then turn it out onto a floured surface and knead for 2 minutes until it forms a smooth dough. You may need to add a little extra flour at this stage.

3 Shape the dough into a round, about 15cm (6in) in diameter. With a sharp knife, slash a cross in the top of the dough to allow the bread to rise easily when baking.

4 Place the dough onto the baking tray and cook in the middle of the oven for 30 minutes to create a good crust. Reduce to 200°C (400°F/Gas 6), and bake for 20 minutes until well risen, golden brown, and a skewer inserted into the middle emerges clean. Transfer to a wire rack and allow it to cool for at least 20 minutes before serving.

STORE The bread will keep, well wrapped in paper, for 3 days.

Cornbread

Cornbread is a traditional American loaf that makes a quick and easy accompaniment to soups and stews.

SERVES 8 | 15–20 MINS | 20–25 MINS

Special equipment

23cm (9in) flameproof cast-iron frying pan or similar-sized loose-bottomed round cake tin

Ingredients

60g (2oz) unsalted butter or bacon dripping, melted and cooled, plus extra for greasing
2 fresh corn cobs, about 200g (7oz) weight of kernels
150g (5½oz) fine yellow cornmeal or polenta
125g (4½oz) strong white bread flour
50g (1¾oz) caster sugar
1 tbsp baking powder
1 tsp salt
2 eggs
250ml (8fl oz) milk

1 Preheat the oven to 220°C (425°F/Gas 7). Oil the pan with butter or dripping. Place in oven.

2 Cut away the kernels from the cobs and scrape out the pulp with the back of the knife.

3 Sift the polenta, flour, sugar, baking powder, and salt into a bowl. Add the corn.

4 In a bowl, whisk together the eggs, melted butter or bacon dripping, and milk.

5 Pour three-quarters of the milk mixture into the flour mixture and stir.

6 Draw in the dry ingredients, adding the remaining milk mixture. Stir just until smooth.

7 Carefully take the hot pan out of the oven and pour in the batter; it should sizzle.

8 Quickly brush the top with butter or bacon dripping. Bake for 20–25 minutes.

9 The bread should shrink from the sides of the pan and a skewer should come out clean.

10 Let the cornbread cool slightly on a wire rack. Serve warm, with soup, chilli con carne, or fried chicken. The cornbread does not keep well but leftovers can be used as a stuffing for roast poultry.

Cornbread variations

Corn Muffins with Roasted Red Pepper

In the spirit of the American West, sweet red pepper is roasted, diced, and stirred into a corn batter. Baking the cornbread in muffin trays makes it easily portable for a picnic, packed lunch, or buffet.

MAKES 12 | 20 MINS | 15–20 MINS

Special equipment
12-hole muffin tin

Ingredients
1 large red pepper
150g (5½oz) fine yellow cornmeal or polenta
125g (4½oz) strong white bread flour
1 tbsp caster sugar
1 tbsp baking powder
1 tsp salt
2 eggs
60g (2oz) unsalted butter or bacon dripping, melted and cooled, plus extra for greasing
250ml (9fl oz) milk

Method

1 Heat the grill on its highest setting. Set the pepper underneath and grill, turning as needed, until the skin blackens and blisters. Put the pepper in a plastic bag, close it, and let cool. Peel off the skin and cut out the core. Cut the pepper in half and scrape out the seeds and ribs. Dice the flesh finely.

2 Preheat the oven to 220°C (425°F/Gas 7). Generously grease the muffin tin and place it in the oven to heat up. Sift the polenta, flour, sugar, baking powder, and salt into a large bowl, and make a well in the centre.

3 In a bowl, whisk together the eggs, melted butter or bacon dripping, and milk. Pour three-quarters of the milk mixture into the well in the flour, and stir. Draw in the dry ingredients, adding the remaining milk mixture, and stirring until smooth. Stir in the diced pepper.

4 Remove the muffin tin from the oven and spoon the batter into the muffin holes. Bake in the oven for 15–20 minutes until they start to shrink from the sides of the holes and a metal skewer inserted in the centre comes out clean. Unmould the muffins and let cool.

PREPARE AHEAD Best served warm from the oven, these can be made 1 day ahead and kept tightly wrapped in paper. If possible, warm gently in the oven before serving.

Southern US-style Cornbread

This quick American cornbread is traditionally served as an accompaniment for a barbecue, soup, or stew. Some authentic Southern recipes omit the honey. ▶

SERVES 8 | 10–15 MINS | 25–35 MINS

Special equipment
18cm (7in) loose-bottomed round cake tin or similar-sized flameproof cast-iron frying pan

Ingredients
250g (9oz) fine cornmeal or polenta, ideally white cornmeal if you can get it
2 tsp baking powder
½ tsp fine salt
2 large eggs
250ml (8fl oz) buttermilk
50g (1¾oz) unsalted butter or bacon dripping, melted and cooled, plus extra for greasing
1 tbsp honey (optional)

Method

1 Preheat the oven to 220°C (425°F/Gas 7). Grease the cake tin or frying pan and place it in the oven to heat up. In a bowl, mix the cornmeal, baking powder, and salt. Whisk together the eggs and buttermilk.

2 Make a well in the centre of the cornmeal mixture and pour in the buttermilk mixture, stirring. Stir in the melted butter or bacon dripping, and honey (if using) and mix.

3 Remove the hot cake tin or frying pan from the oven and pour in the mixture. The tin or pan should be hot enough to make the batter sizzle as it goes in; this is what gives the cornbread its distinctive crust.

4 Bake in the middle of the oven for 20–25 minutes until it has risen, and is browning at the edges. Leave to cool for 5 minutes before turning out and slicing as a side dish.

PREPARE AHEAD Best served warm from the oven, the bread can be made 1 day ahead and kept tightly wrapped. Warm gently in the oven before serving.

ALSO TRY...
Chilli and Coriander Cornbread
Add 1 red chilli, deseeded and finely chopped, and 4 tablespoons finely chopped coriander at the same time as the honey.

BAKER'S TIP
Southern US-style cornbread gains a lot of its flavour from the use of melted bacon dripping in the batter, and a jar of collected leftover bacon grease is a common sight in kitchens across the Southern states of America – so start your own collection!

QUICK BREADS AND BATTERS

Buttermilk Biscuits

A favourite dish of the American South, where they are eaten for breakfast spread with something sweet or to accompany sausage and gravy.

MAKES 12	10 MINS	15 MINS	UP TO 4 WEEKS

Special equipment
6cm (2½in) pastry cutter

Ingredients
250g (9oz) self-raising flour
1 tsp baking powder
½ tsp fine salt
100g (3½oz) unsalted butter, softened
100ml (3½fl oz) buttermilk, plus extra for brushing
1 tbsp runny honey

Method

1 Preheat the oven to 200°C (400°F/Gas 6). Sift the flour and baking powder into a bowl and add the salt. With your fingertips, rub the butter into the dry ingredients until the mixture resembles fine crumbs.

2 Make a well in the centre and pour in the buttermilk and honey. Work the mixture together to form a rough dough, then turn it out onto a lightly floured work surface and bring it together into a smooth ball. Do not over handle it or the biscuits may harden (see Baker's Tip).

3 Roll out the dough to a thickness of 2cm (¾in) and cut 6cm (2½in) biscuits out of it with the pastry cutter. Gather up the remaining dough, re-roll it, and cut out biscuits until all the dough is used up.

4 Place the biscuits on a non-stick baking sheet and brush the tops with buttermilk, to give them a golden finish. Bake in the top third of the oven for 15 minutes until golden brown and well risen. Remove from the oven and cool for 5 minutes on a wire rack before serving, still warm.

STORE The biscuits can be kept in an airtight container for 1 day and warmed up again in the oven before serving.

BAKER'S TIP

Buttermilk biscuits have a tendency to harden and taste tough if overhandled. To avoid this, bring the mix together gently and stop as soon as it forms a dough. When rolling gently, try to cut out as many biscuits from the first rolling as possible, as biscuits from subsequent rollings will be tougher.

American Blueberry Pancakes

Dropping the blueberries on top of the half-cooked pancakes stops the juice leaking out into the pan and burning.

MAKES 30

10 MINS

15–20 MINS

Ingredients

30g (1oz) unsalted butter,
    plus extra for frying and to serve
2 large eggs
200g (7oz) self-raising flour
1 tsp baking powder

40g (1¼oz) caster sugar
250ml (8fl oz) milk
1 tsp vanilla extract
150g (5½oz) blueberries
maple syrup, to serve

1 Melt the butter in a small saucepan and set aside to cool.

2 Crack the eggs into a small bowl and lightly beat with a fork until combined.

3 Sift the flour and baking powder into a bowl, lifting the sieve high above to aerate the flour.

4 Stir in the sugar until evenly mixed with the flour, so each pancake will be equally sweet.

5 In a jug, lightly beat together the milk, eggs, and vanilla extract until well blended.

6 With a spoon, form a well in the centre of the dry ingredients.

7 Pour a little of the egg mixture into the well and start to whisk it in.

8 Wait until each addition of egg mixture has been incorporated before whisking in more.

9 Finally, whisk in the melted butter until the mixture is entirely smooth.

QUICK BREADS AND BATTERS

132

10 Melt a knob of butter in a large, non-stick frying pan over a medium heat.

11 Pour 1 tablespoon of the batter into the pan, to form a round pancake.

12 Continue to add tablespoons of batter, leaving space between for them to spread.

13 As they begin to cook, sprinkle a few blueberries over the uncooked surface.

14 They are ready to turn when small bubbles appear and pop, leaving small holes.

15 Turn the pancakes over carefully with a palette knife.

16 Continue to cook for 1–2 minutes until golden brown on both sides and cooked.

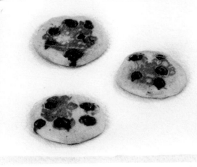

17 Remove the pancakes from the pan, and drain briefly on kitchen paper.

18 Place the pancakes on a plate and transfer to a warm oven.

19 Wipe out the frying pan with kitchen paper, and add another knob of butter.

20 Repeat for all the batter and wipe between batches. The pan should not get too hot.

21 Remove the pancakes from the oven. Serve warm in piles, with butter and maple syrup.

American Pancake variations

Cinnamon Pancakes

Transform any leftover pancakes with this quick topping.

MAKES 8 — 10 MINS — 5 MINS

Ingredients

1 tsp ground cinnamon
4 tbsp caster sugar
8 leftover American pancakes,
  see pages 132–133
25g (scant 1oz) unsalted butter, melted
Greek yogurt, to serve (optional)

Method

1 Preheat the grill on its highest setting. Mix the cinnamon and sugar together, and tip out onto a plate. Brush each cold pancake on both sides with melted butter, and press each side into the sugar and cinnamon mixture, shaking off the excess sugar.

2 Place the pancakes on an oven tray, and cook under the hot grill until the sugar is bubbling and melted. Leave the sugar to set for 1 minute before turning them over and grilling on the other side. Serve immediately with Greek yogurt or just plain as an afternoon snack.

BAKER'S TIP

American pancakes are a great standby, and the recipe is easy to remember once you have cooked it a few times. They can be served as breakfast or dessert, with strawberries, chocolate sauce, or banana and yogurt. Make the toppings as decadent or as healthy as you like.

Drop Scones

So-called because the batter is dropped onto a frying pan.

MAKES 12 — 10 MINS — 15 MINS — UP TO 4 WEEKS

Ingredients

225g (8oz) plain flour
4 tsp baking powder
1 large egg
2 tsp golden syrup
200ml (7fl oz) milk, plus extra if needed
vegetable oil

Method

1 Place a flat griddle pan or large frying pan over medium heat. Fold a tea towel in half and lay it on a baking tray.

2 Sift the flour and baking powder into a bowl. Make a well in the centre and add the egg, golden syrup, and milk. Whisk well to make a smooth batter with the consistency of thick cream. If the mixture is too thick, beat in a little more milk.

3 Test that the griddle pan is hot enough by sprinkling a little flour on the hot surface; it should brown slowly. If it burns, the pan is too hot and needs to cool a little. When the temperature is right, dust off the flour and rub a piece of kitchen towel dipped in cooking oil lightly over the surface. Use oven gloves to protect your hands.

4 Drop a tablespoon of batter from the tip of the spoon onto the pan to make a nice round shape. Repeat, leaving enough room for them to rise and spread.

5 When bubbles appear on the surface of the pancakes, gently flip with a palette knife to cook the other side, pressing lightly with the flat knife to ensure even browning. Place cooked pancakes inside the folded towel to keep them soft, while you fry the rest of the batch.

6 Carefully oil the hot pan after each batch and watch the heat. If the pancakes are cooking too pale, increase the heat; if they brown too quickly, reduce it. Best eaten fresh and warm.

Banana, Yogurt, and Honey Pancake Stack

Try stacking pancakes for a luxurious breakfast treat. ▶

SERVES 6 — 10 MINS — 15–20 MINS

Ingredients

200g (7oz) self-raising flour
1 tsp baking powder
40g (1¼oz) caster sugar
250ml (8fl oz) whole milk
2 large eggs, beaten
½ tsp vanilla extract
30g (1oz) unsalted butter, melted
  and cooled, plus extra for frying
2–3 bananas
200g (7oz) Greek yogurt
runny honey, to serve

Method

1 Sift the flour and baking powder into a large bowl, and add the sugar. In a jug, whisk together the milk, eggs, and vanilla extract. Make a well in the centre of the flour mixture and whisk in the milk mixture, a little at a time. Finally, whisk in the butter until the mixture is entirely smooth.

2 Melt a knob of butter in a large, non-stick frying pan. Pour tablespoons of the batter into the pan, leaving space between them for the pancakes to spread. The pancakes should spread to approximately 8–10cm (3¼–4in) in diameter. Cook the pancakes over medium heat. Turn them over when small bubbles appear on the surface and pop. Cook for another 1–2 minutes until golden brown and cooked through.

3 Slice the bananas on the diagonal to produce 5cm (2in) long strips. Place one warm pancake on a plate, and top with a spoonful of Greek yogurt and some slices of banana. Top with another pancake, more yogurt, and honey. Finish the stack with a third pancake, topped with a spoonful of yogurt and drizzled over generously with runny honey.

Crumpets

Eaten for breakfast or at teatime, toasted crumpets are great with both sweet and savoury toppings.

MAKES 8 | 10 MINS | 20–26 MINS | UP TO 4 WEEKS

Special equipment
4 crumpet rings or 10cm (4in) metal pastry cutters

Ingredients
125g (4½oz) plain flour
125g (4½oz) strong white bread flour
½ tsp dried yeast
175ml (6fl oz) tepid milk
½ tsp salt
½ tsp bicarbonate of soda
vegetable oil, for greasing

Method

1 Mix together the 2 types of flour and yeast. Stir in the milk and 175ml (6fl oz) lukewarm water, and leave for 2 hours or until the bubbles have risen and then started to fall again. Sprinkle the salt and bicarbonate of soda over 2 tablespoons lukewarm water, and whisk into the batter. Set aside for about 5 minutes.

2 Oil the crumpet rings or pastry cutters. Lightly oil a large, heavy frying pan and place the rings in the pan.

3 Pour the batter into a jug. Heat the pan over medium heat, and pour batter into each ring to a depth of 1–2cm (½–¾in).

Cook the crumpets for 8–10 minutes until the batter has set all the way through or holes appear in the top. If no bubbles appear, the mixture is too dry, so stir a little water into the remaining batter.

4 Lift the rings off the crumpets, turn them over, and cook for another 2–3 minutes, or until just golden. Repeat with the remaining batter. Serve the crumpets warm, or toast to reheat if serving them later.

BAKER'S TIP
The holes on top of crumpets are their unique selling point, making them the perfect repository for butter, jam, or marmalade. The leavening creates bubbles as they cook, which burst to produce these holes. Home-made crumpets tend to have fewer holes, but are no less tasty or absorbent for it.

Crêpes Suzette

In this most classic of French desserts, crêpes are flambéd just before serving. A sure way to create culinary drama.

SERVES 6 | 40–50 MINS | 45–60 MINS

Standing time
30 mins

Ingredients

For the crêpes
175g (6oz) plain flour, sifted
1 tbsp caster sugar
½ tsp salt
4 eggs
375ml (13fl oz) milk, plus extra if needed
90g (3oz) unsalted butter, melted and cooled, plus extra if needed

For the orange butter
175g (6oz) unsalted butter, at room temperature
30g (1oz) icing sugar
3 large oranges, 2 finely grated and 1 pared with a vegetable peeler, then cut into julienne strips
1 tbsp Grand Marnier

For flaming
75ml (2½fl oz) brandy
75ml (2½fl oz) Grand Marnier

1 Mix the flour, sugar, and salt. Make a well in the centre. Add the eggs and half the milk.

2 Whisk, drawing in the flour, to make a batter. Whisk in half the butter until smooth.

3 Add milk to give a batter the consistency of single cream. Cover and leave for 30 minutes.

4 For the orange butter, cream together the butter and icing sugar with an electric whisk.

5 With a sharp knife, cut the pith and skin from all 3 oranges.

6 Slide the knife down both sides of each segment to cut it free. Set aside.

7 Add the zest and 2 tablespoons juice to the butter with the Grand Marnier. Whisk well.

8 Add the julienned orange strips to a pan of boiling water, simmer for 2 minutes. Drain.

9 Add a little melted butter to a small frying pan and heat over medium-high heat.

10 Ladle 2–3 tablespoons of the batter into the pan, tilting the pan so the base is covered.

11 Fry for 1 minute. Gently loosen with a palette knife. Turn and cook for 30–60 seconds.

12 Repeat to make 12 crêpes, adding butter only when they start to stick.

13 Spread the orange butter over 1 side of each crêpe. Heat the pan over medium heat.

14 Add 1 crêpe at a time, butter-side down. Cook for 1 minute and fold into quarters.

15 Arrange the crêpes in the hot frying pan. Heat the alcohol, then pour over the crêpes.

16 Stand back. Hold a lighted match to the side of the pan. Baste until the flames die down.

17 Divide the crêpes among warmed plates, and spoon the sauce from the pan over them.

18 Decorate with orange segments and strips, and serve. **PREPARE AHEAD** The plain crêpes can be made 3 days ahead, layered with parchment, and stored, wrapped, in the refrigerator.

Crêpe variations

Buckwheat Galettes

These savoury pancakes are popular in the Brittany region of France, where the local cuisine is defined by rich, rustic flavours

| SERVES 4 | 25 MINS | 25–30 MINS | 12 WEEKS, UNFILLED |

Resting time
2 hrs

Ingredients

For the galettes
75g (2½oz) buckwheat flour
75g (2½oz) plain flour
2 eggs, beaten
250ml (8fl oz) milk
sunflower oil, for greasing

For the filling
2 tbsp sunflower oil
2 red onions, thinly sliced
200g (7oz) smoked ham, chopped
1 tsp thyme leaves
115g (4oz) Brie, cut into small pieces
100ml (3½fl oz) crème fraîche

Method

1 Sift the flour into a large bowl, make a well in the centre, and add the eggs. Gradually beat the eggs into the flour using a wooden spoon, then add the milk and 100ml (3½fl oz) water to make a smooth batter. Cover and let it stand for 2 hours.

2 Heat the oil for the filling in a small frying pan, add the onions, and fry gently until softened. Add the ham and thyme, then remove from the heat and set aside.

3 Preheat the oven to 150°C (300°F/Gas 2). Heat a large frying pan and grease lightly. Spoon in 2 tablespoons of the batter and swirl so it coats the base of the pan. Cook for about 1 minute or until lightly browned underneath, then flip over and cook for another minute or until browned on the other side. Make 7 more galettes, re-greasing the pan as necessary.

4 Stir the Brie and crème fraîche into the filling, and divide it between the crêpes. Then roll or fold them up, and place them on a baking sheet. Heat through in the oven for 10 minutes before serving.

PREPARE AHEAD Make the batter a few hours in advance and leave to stand until ready to cook. If it thickens too much, stir in a little water before using.

Spinach, Pancetta, and Ricotta Pancake Bake

Try making with shop-bought pancakes for a speedy supper.

| SERVES 4 | 30 MINS | 35 MINS | 12 WEEKS, UNBAKED |

Special equipment
25 x 32cm (10 x 12¾in) shallow ovenproof dish

Ingredients

For the batter
175g (6oz) plain flour
½ tsp fine salt
250ml (8fl oz) whole milk, plus extra if needed
4 eggs
50g (1¾oz) unsalted butter, melted and cooled, plus extra for frying and greasing

For the filling
50g (1¾oz) pine nuts
2 tsp extra virgin olive oil
1 red onion, finely chopped
100g (3½oz) diced pancetta
2 garlic cloves, crushed
300g (10½oz) baby spinach, washed and dried
250g (9oz) ricotta
3–4 tbsp double cream
sea salt and freshly ground black pepper

For the cheese sauce
350ml (12fl oz) double cream
60g (2oz) Parmesan cheese, finely grated

Method

1 To make the pancakes, mix the flour and salt in a large bowl. In a separate bowl, whisk together the milk and eggs. Make a well in the centre of the flour mixture and whisk in the milk mixture, a little at a time, until it is all incorporated. Add the butter and whisk until entirely smooth. The mixture should be the consistency of pouring cream. Add a little extra milk if needed. Transfer the batter to a jug, cover with cling film, and leave it to rest for 30 minutes.

2 To make the filling, dry-fry the pine nuts in a large frying pan for a couple of minutes over medium heat, turning them often until they are golden brown in places. Set aside.

QUICK BREADS AND BATTERS

3 Add the olive oil to the pan and sauté the onion for 3 minutes until softened, but not browned. Add the pancetta and fry it over medium heat for another 5 minutes until golden brown and crispy. Add the garlic and cook for another minute. Add the baby spinach in handfuls. The spinach will wilt very quickly, so cook only until it begins to wilt, then remove the pan from the heat.

4 Tip the spinach mixture into a sieve, and press down with the back of a spoon to remove excess water. Tip it into a bowl, add the pine nuts, and mix it all with the ricotta and the cream. Season well and set aside.

5 Melt a knob of butter in a large, non-stick frying pan, and when it begins to sizzle wipe away any excess with a piece of kitchen paper. Pour a ladleful of the pancake mixture into the frying pan and then tip the pan to cover with a thin layer of the batter. Cook for 2 minutes on each side, turning them when the first side is golden brown. Set the cooked pancakes aside and continue until all the batter has been used up, adding a knob more butter when necessary. This should make 10 pancakes.

6 Preheat the oven to 200°C (400°F/Gas 6). Lay a pancake out flat. Put 2 tablespoons of filling into the middle of the pancake. Use the back of the spoon to spread it out into a thick line, then roll the pancake up around it. Grease the dish, and lay the pancakes side by side in the dish.

7 For the sauce, heat the double cream until nearly boiling. Add nearly all the Parmesan. Whisk until the cheese melts, then bring to a boil and simmer for a couple of minutes until it thickens slightly. Season to taste and pour over the pancakes. Top with the reserved cheese.

8 Bake at the top of the oven for 20 minutes until golden brown and bubbling in places. Remove from the oven and serve at once.

PREPARE AHEAD This can be made up to the end of step 6, covered, and refrigerated for up to 2 days, before finishing with the sauce and baking as described.

Swedish Pancake Stack Cake

Make sure you use only the thinnest of crêpes for this sumptuous dessert – a perfect summer birthday cake and a children's favourite.

SERVES 6–8 | 10 MINS | 15 MINS

Ingredients
6 pancakes, made using ½ quantity crêpe batter, see pages 140–141, steps 1–3 and 10–12
200ml (7fl oz) double cream
250ml (8fl oz) crème fraîche
3 tbsp caster sugar
¼ tsp vanilla extract
250g (9oz) raspberries
icing sugar, to serve

Method

1 Whip the double cream to form stiff peaks. Mix the cream, crème fraîche, caster sugar, and vanilla extract, and whisk until well blended. Reserve about 4 tablespoons to decorate the top of the cake.

2 Set aside a handful of the raspberries. Lightly crush the remaining fruit with a fork, and add them to the remaining cream mixture, folding them through roughly to create a rippled effect.

3 Place 1 pancake on a platter, spread one-fifth of the cream over it, and top with a second pancake. Continue to layer until all the pancakes and cream are used up.

4 Decorate the top with the reserved cream mixture, scatter the remaining raspberries over the top, dust with icing sugar and serve.

BAKER'S TIP
This stack cake is extremely versatile. Try using chopped strawberries or blueberries, which will make an equally delicious cake. In Sweden, lingonberry jam (similar to sweet cranberry sauce) is often used as a substitute for the fresh fruit. Look for the jam in Scandinavian delicatessens.

Staffordshire Oatcakes

These oat pancakes can have sweet or savoury fillings, can be folded in half, rolled up, or cooked on top of each other, then sliced in quarters.

MAKES 10 | **10 MINS** | **15 MINS**

Resting time
1–2 hrs

Ingredients
200g (7oz) fine oatmeal
100g (3½oz) wholemeal flour
100g (3½oz) plain flour
½ tsp fine salt
2 tsp dried yeast
300ml (10fl oz) milk
unsalted butter, for frying

For the filling
250g (9oz) cheese, such as Cheddar
  or Red Leicester, grated
20 slices streaky bacon

Method

1 Sift together the fine oatmeal, wholemeal flour, plain flour, and salt. Add the dried yeast to 400ml (14fl oz) warm water and whisk well until it is completely dissolved. Add the milk. Make a well in the centre of the dry ingredients, and stir in the milk and water mixture.

2 Whisk the mixture together until the batter is completely smooth. Cover and set aside for 1–2 hours until small bubbles start to appear on the surface of the batter.

3 Melt a knob of butter in a large, non-stick frying pan and when it begins to sizzle, wipe any excess away quickly with a piece of kitchen paper.

4 Pour a ladleful of the oatcake mixture into the centre of the frying pan, and then tip the pan to allow the batter to spread all around. The idea is to cover the surface of the pan as quickly as possible with a thin layer of the oatcake batter.

5 Cook the oatcakes for 2 minutes on each side, turning them when the edges are cooked through and the first side is golden brown. Set the cooked oatcakes aside in a warm place and continue until all the batter has been used up.

6 Meanwhile, preheat the grill on its highest setting, and grill the streaky bacon. Sprinkle a handful of grated cheese all over the surface of an oatcake.

7 Place it under the grill for 1–2 minutes until the cheese has completely melted. Place 2 slices of grilled streaky bacon on top of the melted cheese to one side of the oatcake, roll it up, and serve.

BAKER'S TIP
These traditional oatcakes are really savoury pancakes, though a little more wholesome, and make a fantastic breakfast treat every once in a while. For an even quicker breakfast, the batter can be made the night before and stored, covered, in the refrigerator overnight.

STAFFORDSHIRE OATCAKES

145

Blinis

These buckwheat-based pancakes originated in Russia. Try serving them as canapés, or larger topped with smoked fish and crème fraîche for lunch.

MAKES 48 BLINIS | 20 MINS | 15 MINS | UP TO 8 WEEKS

Resting time
2 hrs

Ingredients
½ tsp dried yeast
200ml (7fl oz) warm milk
100g (3½ oz) soured cream
100g (3½oz) buckwheat flour
100g (3½oz) strong white bread flour
½ tsp fine salt
2 eggs, separated
50g (1¾oz) unsalted butter, melted and cooled, plus extra for frying
soured cream, smoked salmon, chives, and freshly ground pepper, to serve (optional)

Method

1 Mix the yeast with the warm milk, and whisk until the yeast dissolves. Whisk in the soured cream and set aside.

2 In a large bowl, mix together the 2 types of flour and the salt. Make a well in the centre and gradually whisk in the milk and soured cream. Add the egg yolks and continue to whisk. Finally, add the butter and whisk until smooth.

3 Cover the bowl with cling film and keep in a warm place for at least 2 hours until bubbles appear all over the surface.

4 In a clean bowl, whisk the egg whites to form soft peaks. Add the egg whites to the batter and gently fold them in using a metal spoon or spatula, until they are well combined and there are no lumps of egg white. Transfer the batter to a jug.

5 Heat a knob of butter in a large, non-stick frying pan. Pour the batter into the pan, 1 tablespoon at a time, to form small blinis, about 6cm (2½in) in diameter. Cook the blinis for 1–2 minutes over medium heat until bubbles start to appear on the surface. When the bubbles begin to pop, turn and cook for another minute on the second side. Transfer the blinis to a warm plate, cover with a clean tea towel, and continue to cook them until all the batter is used up. Add another knob of butter to the pan occasionally, if it gets dry.

6 Serve the blinis soon after cooking or while still warm, with soured cream and smoked salmon, seasoned with plenty of black pepper and topped with snipped chives, for delicious canapés. They can also be wrapped in foil and gently reheated in a medium oven for 10 minutes before serving.

PREPARE AHEAD The blinis can be made up to 3 days ahead of time and kept in an airtight container in the refrigerator. Reheat from fresh or frozen as in step 6.

BAKER'S TIP
Blinis are simple to make, but can be difficult to get perfectly circular and small enough to serve as a canapé. Remember to pour the batter directly into the centre of the blini and use a spoon to catch any drips from the jug as you finish pouring.

QUICK BREADS AND BATTERS

Cherry Clafoutis

This French dessert combines sweetened egg custard and ripe fruit, baked until set and the fruit is bursting.

SERVES 6 **12 MINS** **35–45 MINS**

Resting time
30 mins

Special equipment
25cm (10in) tart tin or ovenproof dish

Ingredients
750g (1lb 10oz) cherries
3 tbsp Kirsch
75g (2½oz) caster sugar
unsalted butter, for greasing
4 large eggs
1 vanilla pod or 1 tsp vanilla extract
100g (3½oz) plain flour

300ml (10fl oz) milk
pinch of salt
icing sugar, for dusting
thick cream, crème fraîche,
  or vanilla ice cream, to serve
  (optional)

1 Toss the cherries with the Kirsch and 2 tablespoons sugar. Leave for 30 minutes.

2 Preheat the oven to 200°C (400°F/Gas 6). Butter the flan tin, and set aside.

3 Strain the Kirsch from the cherries into a large bowl. Set the cherries aside.

4 Beat the eggs and vanilla extract (if using) into the Kirsch, until thoroughly combined.

5 With a sharp knife, split the vanilla pod (if using) vertically down the middle.

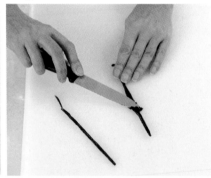

6 Run the tip of the knife down the middle of each half to scrape out all the seeds.

7 Add the seeds to the egg and Kirsch mixture and mix well to distribute.

8 Add the remaining sugar and beat well to combine.

9 Sift the flour into a large bowl, lifting the sieve high to aerate the flour as it floats down.

10 Beat the flour into the egg mixture, whisking after each addition, to make a smooth paste.

11 Pour in the milk, add the salt, and whisk until it makes a smooth batter.

12 Arrange the cherries in 1 layer in the flan dish. They should fill the dish.

13 Slowly pour the batter over the top of the cherries, trying not to displace the cherries.

14 Bake for 35–45 minutes or until the top is browned and the centre is firm to the touch.

15 Allow to cool on a wire rack, then remove from the tin and dust with icing sugar.

16 Serve warm or at room temperature, with plenty of thick cream or crème fraîche for spooning over, or with vanilla ice cream.

Clafoutis variations

Toad in the Hole

This savoury British version of clafoutis is perfect comfort food.

SERVES 4   **20 MINS**   **35–40 MINS**

Standing time
30 mins

Special equipment
Roasting tin or shallow ovenproof dish

Ingredients
125g (4½oz) plain flour
pinch of salt
2 eggs
300ml (10fl oz) milk
2 tbsp vegetable oil
8 good-quality sausages

Method

1 To make the batter, put the flour into a bowl with the salt, make a well in the centre, and add the eggs with a little of the milk. Whisk together, gradually incorporating the flour. Add the remaining milk and whisk to make a smooth batter. Leave to rest for at least 30 minutes.

2 Preheat the oven to 220°C (425°F/Gas 7). Heat the oil in a roasting tin or shallow ovenproof dish. Add the sausages and toss them in the hot oil. Bake for 5–10 minutes or until the sausages are just coloured and the fat is very hot.

3 Reduce the oven temperature to 200°C (400°F/Gas 6). Carefully pour the batter around the sausages and return to the oven for a further 30 minutes or until the batter is risen, golden, and crisp. Serve immediately.

PREPARE AHEAD The batter can be made 24 hours in advance. Keep chilled and whisk briefly just before using.

Apricot Clafoutis

This French favourite can be enjoyed warm or at room temperature. Tinned apricots taste just fine, when fresh are out of season.

SERVES 4   **10 MINS**   **35 MINS**

Special equipment
shallow ovenproof dish

Ingredients
unsalted butter, for greasing
250g (9oz) fresh ripe apricots, halved and pitted or 1 tin of apricot halves, drained
1 egg, plus 1 egg yolk
25g (scant 1oz) plain flour
50g (1¾oz) caster sugar
150ml (5fl oz) double cream
¼ tsp vanilla extract
thick cream or crème fraîche, to serve (optional)

Method

1 Preheat the oven to 200°C (400°F/Gas 6). Lightly grease the dish; it should be big enough to fit the apricots in a single layer. Place the apricots cut-side down in a single layer in the dish; there should be space between them.

2 In a bowl, whisk together the egg, egg yolk, and the flour. Whisk in the caster sugar. Finally, add the cream and vanilla extract, and whisk thoroughly to form a smooth custard.

3 Pour the custard around the apricots, so the tops of a few are just visible. Bake in the top shelf of the oven for 35 minutes until puffed up and golden brown in places. Remove and let cool for at least 15 minutes. It is best served warm, with thick cream or crème fraîche.

PREPARE AHEAD The clafoutis is best freshly baked and served warm, but can be cooked up to 6 hours ahead and served at room temperature.

QUICK BREADS AND BATTERS

Plum and Marzipan Clafoutis

This stunning version is equally good made with damsons or cherries, but instead of putting the marzipan in the fruit cavities, dot little pieces between each fruit.

SERVES
6

30
MINS

50
MINS

Special equipment
shallow ovenproof dish

Ingredients

For the marzipan
115g (4oz) ground almonds
60g (2oz) caster sugar
60g (2oz) icing sugar, plus extra for dusting
few drops of almond extract
½ tsp lemon juice
1 egg white, lightly beaten

For the clafoutis
675g (1½lb) plums, halved and stoned
75g (2½oz) butter
4 eggs and 1 egg yolk
115g (4oz) caster sugar
85g (3oz) plain flour, sifted
450ml (15fl oz) milk
150ml (5fl oz) single cream

Method
1 Preheat the oven to 190°C (375°F/Gas 5). Mix the marzipan ingredients together with enough of the egg white to form a stiff paste. Push a tiny piece of the paste into the cavity in each plum half.

2 Grease a shallow, ovenproof dish, large enough to hold the plums in a single layer, with 15g (½oz) of the butter. Arrange the plums cut-side down in the dish, with the marzipan underneath. Melt the remaining butter and leave to cool.

3 Add any leftover egg white from the marzipan to the eggs and egg yolk. Add the sugar and whisk until thick and pale. Whisk in the melted butter, flour, milk, and cream to form a batter. Pour over the plums and bake in the oven for about 50 minutes until golden and just set. Serve warm, dusted with icing sugar.

PREPARE AHEAD The clafoutis is best freshly baked and served warm, but can be cooked 6 hours ahead and served at room temperature.

BAKER'S TIP
Clafoutis is basically a sweetened custard, baked around any type of seasonal fruit. As a storecupboard standby, try this version with tinned apricots, but in season, you can use cherries, blackberries, plums, and black, white, or redcurrants.

Plum Clafoutis

This is a satisfying autumn dessert to make when the plums are at their peak. You can substitute the Kirsch for plum or ordinary brandy, if preferred. **PICTURED OVERLEAF**

SERVES
6–8

20–25
MINS

30–35
MINS

Special equipment
shallow ovenproof dish

Ingredients
unsalted butter, for greasing
100g (3½oz) caster sugar,
  plus extra for baking dish
625g (1lb 5oz) small plums, halved and pitted
45g (1½oz) plain flour
pinch of salt
150ml (5fl oz) milk
75ml (2½fl oz) double cream
4 eggs, plus 2 egg yolks
3 tbsp Kirsch
2 tbsp icing sugar
whipped cream, to serve (optional)

Method
1 Preheat the oven to 180°C (350°F/Gas 4). Grease the baking dish. Sprinkle over some sugar, and turn it around to coat the bottom and sides evenly. Tip out any excess. Spread the plums, cut-side up, in an even layer.

2 Sift the flour and salt into a bowl. Make a well in the centre, and pour in the milk and cream. Whisk, drawing in the flour, to make a smooth paste. Add the eggs, egg yolks, and caster sugar, and whisk to make a smooth batter.

3 Just before baking, ladle the batter over the plums, then spoon over the Kirsch. Bake for 30–35 minutes until puffed up and beginning to brown. Just before serving, sift over the icing sugar. Serve warm or at room temperature, with whipped cream.

PREPARE AHEAD The clafoutis is best freshly baked and served warm, but can be cooked 6 hours ahead and served at room temperature.

sweet breads

Brioche des rois

This French bread is traditionally eaten at Epiphany, 6th January. The *fève* represents the gifts of the Three Kings.

SERVES 10–12

25 MINS

25–30 MINS

UP TO 4 WEEKS

Rising and proving time
4–6 hrs

Special equipment
25cm (10in) ring mould (optional)
fève porcelain or metal trinket
(optional; see Baker's Tip, page 159)

Ingredients

For the brioche
2½ tsp dried yeast
2 tbsp caster sugar
5 eggs, beaten
375g (13oz) strong white bread
flour, plus extra for dusting
1½ tsp salt
oil, for greasing
175g (6oz) unsalted butter,
cubed and softened

For the topping
1 egg, lightly beaten
50g (1¾oz) mixed candied fruit
(orange and lemon zest, glacé
cherries, and angelica), chopped
25g (scant 1oz) coarse sugar
crystals (optional)

1 Whisk the yeast, 2 tablespoons warm water, and sugar. Leave for 10 minutes. Add eggs.

2 In a large bowl, sift together the flour and salt, and add the remaining sugar.

3 Make a well in the flour and pour in the eggs and yeast mixture.

4 Use a fork and then your hands to bring the dough together; it will be quite sticky.

5 Turn out the dough onto a lightly floured work surface.

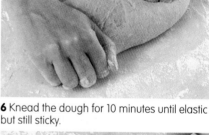

6 Knead the dough for 10 minutes until elastic but still sticky.

7 Put in an oiled bowl and cover with cling film. Leave to rise in a warm place for 2–3 hours.

8 Gently knock the dough back on a lightly floured work surface.

9 Scatter one-third of the cubed butter over the surface of the dough.

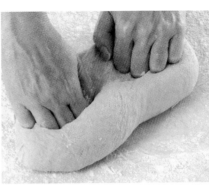

10 Fold the dough over the butter and knead gently for 5 minutes.

11 Repeat until all the butter is absorbed. Keep kneading until no streaks of butter show.

12 Form into a round and work it into a ring. Bury the *fève*, if using (see Baker's Tip, page 159).

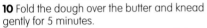

13 Transfer to an oiled baking sheet or fill an oiled ring mould (if using).

14 If you don't have a ring mould, use a ramekin to keep the shape of the hole.

15 Cover with cling film and a tea towel. Leave to prove for 2–3 hours until doubled in size.

16 Brush the brioche with beaten egg. Sprinkle over candied fruit and sugar crystals (if using).

17 Preheat the oven to 200°C (400°F/Gas 6). Bake for 25–30 minutes until golden brown.

18 Leave to cool slightly, then turn out onto a wire rack, without dislodging the toppings.
STORE This will keep in an airtight container for 3 days.

Brioche variations

Brioche Buns

These bite-sized little buns are known in French as *brioche à tête*, for obvious reasons.

MAKES 10 BUNS	45–50 MINS	15–20 MINS	UP TO 8 WEEKS

Rising and proving time
1½–2 hrs

Special equipment
10 x 7.5cm (3in) brioche moulds

Ingredients
butter, melted, for greasing
1 quantity brioche dough,
  see pages 156–157, steps 1–11
flour, for dusting
1 egg, beaten, for glazing
½ tsp salt, for glazing

Method

1 Brush the brioche moulds with melted butter and set them on a baking sheet.

2 Divide the dough in half. Roll 1 piece of dough into a cylinder, 5cm (2in) in diameter, and cut it into 5 pieces. Repeat with the remaining dough. Roll each piece of dough into a smooth ball.

3 Pinch one-quarter of each ball, almost dividing it from the remaining dough, to form the head. Holding the head, lower each ball into a mould, twisting and pressing the head onto the base. Cover with a dry tea towel and leave to prove in a warm place for 30 minutes.

4 Preheat the oven to 220°C (425°F/Gas 7). Mix the egg and salt for glazing. Brush the brioches with egg glaze. Bake for 15–20 minutes until brown and hollow sounding when tapped; unmould and cool on a wire rack.

STORE These will keep in an airtight container for 3 days.

Rum Babas

Boozy, cake-like versions of brioche buns – perfect for a dinner party.

MAKES 4 BABAS	20 MINS	20 MINS

Rising time
30 mins

Special equipment
4 x 7.5cm (3in) brioche moulds or baba tins

For the babas
60g (2oz) butter, melted, plus extra for greasing
150g (5½oz) strong plain flour
60g (2oz) raisins
1½ tsp fast-action dried yeast
155g (5½oz) caster sugar
pinch of salt
2 eggs, lightly beaten
4 tbsp milk, warmed
vegetable oil, for greasing
3 tbsp rum
300ml (10fl oz) whipping cream
2 tbsp icing sugar
grated chocolate, to serve

Method

1 Grease the moulds with butter. Place the flour in a bowl and stir in the raisins, yeast, 30g (1oz) sugar, and salt. Beat together the egg and milk, and add to the flour mixture. Stir in the butter. Beat well for 3–4 minutes, then pour into the moulds to half fill them.

2 Place the moulds on a baking tray and cover with a sheet of oiled cling film. Leave to rise in a warm place for 30 minutes, or until doubled in size and filling the moulds. Preheat the oven to 200°C (400°F/Gas 6). Bake for 10–15 minutes until golden. Leave to cool on a wire rack. If freezing, do so at this stage.

3 Heat 120ml (4fl oz) of water in a pan with the remaining sugar, boiling rapidly for 2 minutes. Remove from the heat and cool. Stir in the rum. Pierce holes in the babas using a skewer, then dip them in the syrup.

4 Before serving, pour the cream into a bowl, add the icing sugar, and whisk until peaks form. Place a dollop of cream on each baba, sprinkle over chocolate, and serve.

Brioche Nanterre

Basic brioche dough can be baked into rings, buns, or loaves. This classic brioche loaf is best for slicing and fantastic toasted.

| MAKES 1 LOAF | 30 MINS | 30 MINS | UP TO 4 WEEKS |

Rising and proving time
4–6 hrs

Special equipment
900g (2lb) loaf tin

Ingredients
1 quantity brioche dough,
see pages 156–157, steps 1–11
1 egg, beaten, for glazing

Method

1 Line the bottom and sides of the tin with parchment. Put a double layer on the base. Divide the dough into 8 pieces, and roll them up to form small balls. They should fit in pairs, side by side, in the base of the prepared tin.

2 Cover with cling film and a tea towel, and leave to prove for a further 2–3 hours until the dough has again doubled in size.

3 Preheat the oven to 200°C (400°F/Gas 6). Brush the top of the brioche loaf with a little beaten egg, and bake near the top of the oven for 30 minutes or until the bottom of the loaf sounds hollow when tapped. Check the loaf after 20 minutes and cover the top with a piece of loose-fitting parchment if it is in danger of becoming too brown.

4 Leave to cool in the tin for a few minutes, then turn out onto a wire rack to cool. This brioche is delicious toasted and buttered.

STORE The loaf will keep in an airtight container for 3 days.

BAKER'S TIP

Brioche originated in France and was baked to celebrate Epiphany on 6 January. Traditionally, a *fève* is hidden in the dough, and the finder is guaranteed luck for the coming year. In the past, a dried bean or *fève* was used, but these days small decorative ceramic figures are more common.

Hefezopf

This traditional German bread is similar to brioche. Like all yeasted sweet breads, it is at its best the day of baking.

| MAKES 1 LOAF | 20 MINS | 25–35 MINS | UP TO 8 WEEKS |

Rising and proving time
4–4½ hrs

Ingredients
2 tsp dried yeast
125ml (4fl oz) warm milk
1 large egg
450g (1lb) plain flour,
  plus extra for dusting
75g (2½oz) caster sugar
¼ tsp fine salt

75g (2½oz) unsalted butter, melted
vegetable oil, for greasing
1 egg, beaten, for glazing

1 Dissolve the yeast in the warm milk. Let it cool, then add the egg and beat well.

2 Put the flour, sugar, and salt in a large bowl. Make a well and pour in the milk mixture.

3 Add the melted butter and gradually draw in the flour, stirring to form a soft dough.

4 Knead for 10 minutes on a floured surface until smooth, soft, and pliable.

5 Put in an oiled bowl and cover with cling film. Keep it warm for 2–2½ hours until doubled.

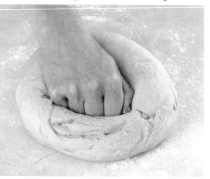

6 Put the dough on a floured work surface and gently knock it back. Divide into 3 equal pieces.

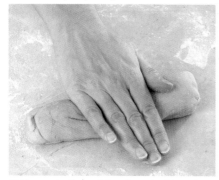

7 Take each piece of dough and roll it under your palm to make a fat log shape.

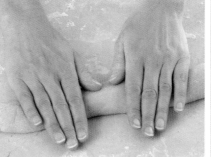

8 Using your palms, continue to roll it towards each end, until it is about 30cm (12in) long.

9 Pinch the tops of the 3 pieces together and tuck the join underneath to start the plait.

SWEET BREADS

10 Loosely plait the dough, leaving room for it to rise. Pinch and tuck the ends underneath.

11 Put on a baking sheet lined with parchment. Cover with oiled cling film and a tea towel.

12 Leave in a warm place for 2 hours; it will not double now, but will rise on baking.

13 Preheat the oven to 190°C (375°F/Gas 5). Brush liberally with beaten egg.

14 Bake for 25–30 minutes until golden. Check if undercooked where the plaits meet.

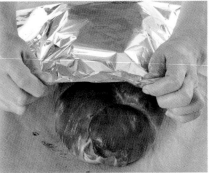

15 If undercooked, cover with foil and bake for 5 minutes. Cool for 15 minutes before serving.

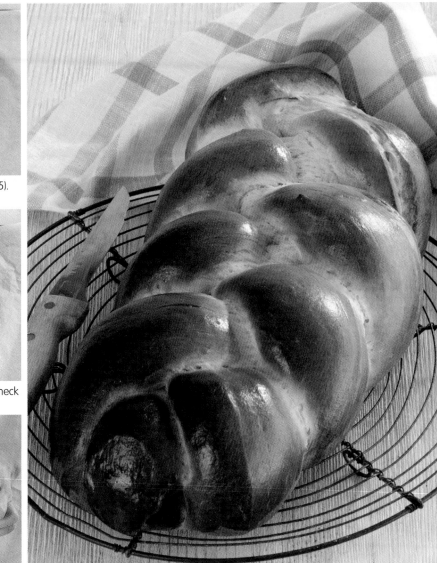

STORE Wrap in cling film for up to 2 days. **ALSO TRY... Sultana and Almond Hefezopf** Add 75g (2½oz) golden sultanas at step 2 and scatter 2 tablespoons flaked almonds at step 13.

Hefezopf variations

Spiced Pecan and Raisin Hefezopf

The nuts and spices make this bread even tastier toasted.

| MAKES 1 LOAF | 30 MINS | 25–35 MINS | UP TO 8 WEEKS |

Rising and proving time
4–4½ hrs

Ingredients
3 x "logs" hefezopf dough, approx. 30cm (12in)
  long, see page 160, steps 1–8
50g (1¾oz) raisins
50g (1¾oz) pecans, roughly chopped
3 tbsp soft light brown sugar
2 tsp mixed spice

Method

1 Roll each "log" of dough out on its shorter edge, so that you have 3 pieces each 30 x 8cm (12 x 3¼in). The measurements do not have to be precise, but the pieces of dough should be roughly the same shape.

2 Mix together the raisins, pecans, sugar, and mixed spice. Scatter one-third of the mixture over each piece of dough, and press down with your palms firmly. Roll up each piece along its longest side, tucking the dough in firmly as you go. You should be left with three 30cm (12in) "ropes" of dough stuffed with the raisin and nut mix.

3 Pinch the tops of the 3 pieces of dough together and tuck the join underneath. Now loosely plait the dough together, leaving room for it to rise, and pinch and tuck the ends underneath.

4 Transfer the loaf to a baking sheet lined with baking parchment, cover with lightly oiled cling film and a tea towel, and leave in a warm place for a further 2 hours. This dough will rise, but not double in size. Preheat the oven to 190°C (375°F/Gas 5).

5 Brush the loaf with egg, making sure to get into the joins of the plait. Bake in the preheated oven for 25–30 minutes until well risen and golden brown. If the bread is undercooked where the plaits meet, but

has browned well, cover loosely with foil and cook for a further 5 minutes. Remove from the oven and leave to cool on a wire rack for at least 15 minutes before serving.

STORE The loaf is best eaten the day it is made, but will store, wrapped in cling film, for 2 days.

BAKER'S TIP

Hefezopf is a sweet yeasted bread, traditionally plaited and baked at Easter all over Germany. It is quite similar to a brioche dough recipe, and can be baked plain or stuffed with a variety of dried fruits and nuts. Try experimenting with this recipe to include your favourites.

SWEET BREADS

Challah

This traditional Jewish bread is
baked for holidays and the Sabbath.

MAKES | **45–55** | **35–40** | **UP TO 8**
1 LOAF | **MINS** | **MINS** | **WEEKS**

Proving time
1¾-2¼ hrs

Ingredients
2½ tsp dried yeast
4 tbsp vegetable oil, plus extra for greasing
4 tbsp sugar
2 eggs, plus 1 yolk, for glazing
2 tsp salt
550g (1¼lb) strong white bread flour,
  plus extra for dusting
1 tsp poppy seeds, for sprinkling (optional)

Method

1 Put 250ml (8fl oz) of water into a pan and
bring just to a boil. Pour 4 tablespoons into
a bowl, and let cool to lukewarm. Sprinkle
over the yeast and let stand, stirring once,
for 5 minutes, until dissolved. Add the oil
and sugar to the remaining water in the pan
and heat until melted. Let cool to lukewarm.

2 In a large bowl, beat the eggs just until
mixed. Add the cooled sweetened water,
salt, and dissolved yeast. Stir in half the
flour and mix well. Add the remaining flour
gradually, until the dough forms a ball.
It should be soft and slightly sticky.

3 Turn onto a floured work surface.
Knead for 5–7 minutes until very smooth
and elastic. Oil a large bowl. Put the dough
in the bowl, and flip it. Cover with a damp
tea towel and let rise in a warm place for
1–1½ hours until doubled in bulk.

4 Lightly brush a baking sheet with oil.
Turn the dough on to a lightly floured work
surface and knock back. Cut the dough into
4 equal pieces. Flour the work surface. Roll
each piece of dough with your hands to
a 63cm (25in) strand.

5 Line the strands up next to each other.
Starting from your left, lift the first strand to
cross over the second. Lift the third strand
to cross over the fourth. Now lift the fourth

strand and lay it between the first and
second strands. Finish plaiting the strands,
pinching the ends together and tucking
them under the plaited loaf.

6 Transfer the loaf to the prepared baking
sheet. Cover with a dry tea towel and let rise
in a warm place for about 45 minutes until
doubled in bulk. Preheat the oven to 190°C
(375°F/Gas 5). Make the glaze by beating
the egg yolk with 1 tablespoon water until
it looks frothy. Brush the loaf with the glaze,
and sprinkle with poppy seeds, if you like.

7 Bake in the oven for 35–40 minutes until
golden and the bread sounds hollow when
the bottom is tapped.

STORE Challah is best eaten the day it is
made, but will store, wrapped in cling film,
for up to 2 days.

Pane al latte

This soft, slightly sweet Italian milk bread is perfect for small children – though adults will enjoy it for breakfast or afternoon tea as well!

MAKES 1 LOAF | 30 MINS | 20 MINS

Rising and proving time
2½–3 hrs

Ingredients

500g (1lb 2oz) plain flour, plus extra for dusting
1 tsp salt
2 tbsp caster sugar
2 tsp dried yeast
200ml (7fl oz) warm milk
2 eggs, plus 1 egg, beaten, for glazing
50g (1¾oz) unsalted butter, melted
vegetable oil, for greasing

Method

1 Put the flour, salt, and sugar into a bowl and mix well. Dissolve the yeast in the milk, whisking to help it dissolve. Once the liquid has cooled, add the eggs and beat well.

2 Gradually pour the milk mixture, then the butter, into the flour mixture, stirring it to form a soft dough. Knead the dough for 10 minutes on a floured work surface until smooth, glossy, and elastic.

3 Put the dough in a lightly oiled bowl, cover loosely with cling film, and leave to rise in a warm place for up to 2 hours until doubled in size. Turn the dough out onto a lightly floured work surface and gently knock it back. Divide it into 5 roughly equal pieces. Ideally, 2 should be slightly bigger than the rest.

4 Knead each piece briefly, and roll it out to a long, fat log shape – the 3 smaller pieces about 20cm (8in) long, and the 2 larger ones about 25cm (10in) long. Take the 3 shorter pieces and position them side by side on a baking sheet lined with baking parchment. Place the 2 larger ones on each side and draw the tops and bottoms together around the central 3 to form a "circle". Pinch the top of the loaf together to ensure the dough does not come apart.

5 Cover it loosely with lightly oiled cling film and a clean tea towel, and leave it in a warm place to rise for 30 minutes–1 hour until almost doubled in size. Preheat the oven to 190°C (375°F/Gas 5).

6 Gently brush with a little beaten egg and bake for 20 minutes until golden brown. Remove from the oven and leave to cool for at least 10 minutes before serving.

STORE Best eaten still warm from the oven, the bread can be wrapped overnight and toasted the next day.

BAKER'S TIP

The use of eggs, milk, and sugar give this very soft Italian bread a sweet, gentle flavour and velvety texture. It toasts well, but is at its best served still warm with plenty of cold, unsalted butter and home-made strawberry jam. It is especially popular with children.

Panettone

A sweet bread eaten all over Italy at Christmas. Making one is not as hard as it seems and the results are delicious.

SERVES 8 | 30 MINS | 40–45 MINS | UP TO 4 WEEKS

Rising and proving time
4 hrs

Special equipment
15cm (6in) round springform cake tin
  or high-sided panettone tin

Ingredients
2 tsp dried yeast
125ml (4fl oz) milk, warmed in a pan
  and left to cool to lukewarm
50g (1¾oz) caster sugar
425g (15oz) strong white bread flour,
  plus extra for dusting
large pinch of salt
75g (2½oz) unsalted butter, melted
2 large eggs, plus 1 small egg,
  beaten, for brushing
1½ tsp vanilla extract
175g (6oz) mixed dried fruit
  (apricots, cranberries, sultanas,
  mixed peel)
finely grated zest of 1 orange
vegetable oil, for greasing
icing sugar, for dusting

1 Add the yeast to the warm milk in a jug. Mix the sugar, flour, and salt in a large bowl.

2 Once the yeasted milk is frothy (5 minutes), whisk in the butter, large eggs, and vanilla.

3 Mix the liquid and dry ingredients to form a soft dough; it will be stickier than bread dough.

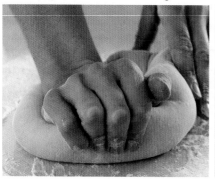

4 On a lightly floured surface, knead the dough for about 10 minutes until elastic.

5 Form the dough into a loose ball and stretch it out flat onto a floured work surface.

6 Scatter the dried fruit and orange zest on top and knead again until well combined.

7 Form the dough into a loose ball and put it in a lightly oiled bowl.

8 Cover the bowl with a damp, clean tea towel or place inside a large plastic bag.

9 Leave the dough to prove in a warm place for up to 2 hours until doubled in size.

10 Line the tin with a double layer of baking parchment or a single layer of silicone paper.

11 If using a cake tin, form a collar with the paper, 5–10cm (2–4in) higher than the tin.

12 Knock the air out of the dough with your fist and turn out onto a lightly floured surface.

13 Knead the dough into a round ball just big enough to fit into the tin.

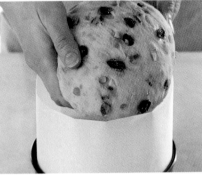

14 Put it into the tin, cover, and leave to prove for another 2 hours until doubled in size.

15 Preheat the oven to 190°C (375°F/Gas 5). Brush the top of the dough with eggwash.

16 Bake in the middle of the oven for 40–45 minutes. If it's browning fast, cover with foil.

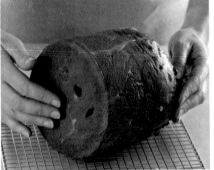

17 The bottom will sound hollow when ready. Leave to cool for 5 minutes, then turn out.

18 Remove the parchment and cool completely on a wire rack before dusting with icing sugar to serve. **STORE** The panettone will keep in an airtight container for 2 days.

Panettone variations

Chocolate and Hazelnut Panettone

This variation of the classic panettone is a sure-fire winner with children and any leftovers can be used to make a particularly delicious Bread and Butter Pudding (see recipe below).

| SERVES 8 | 30 MINS | 45–50 MINS | UP TO 4 WEEKS |

Rising and proving time
3 hrs

Special equipment
15cm (6in) round springform cake tin or high-sided panettone tin

Ingredients
2 tsp dried yeast
125ml (4fl oz) milk, warmed in a pan and left to cool to lukewarm
50g (1¾oz) caster sugar
425g (15oz) strong white bread flour, plus extra for dusting
large pinch of salt
75g (2½oz) unsalted butter, melted
2 large eggs, plus 1 small egg, beaten, for glazing
1 tsp vanilla extract
75g (2½oz) hazelnuts, roughly chopped
finely grated zest of 1 orange
vegetable oil, for greasing
100g (3½oz) dark chocolate chunks, chopped
icing sugar, for dusting

Method

1 In a jug, add the yeast to the warm milk and leave for about 5 minutes, stirring once, until frothy. Combine the sugar, flour, and salt in a mixing bowl. Add the butter, large eggs, and vanilla extract to the yeasted milk, and whisk to combine.

2 Mix the milk mixture with the dry ingredients to form a soft dough. Knead for 10 minutes until smooth and elastic.

3 Stretch out the dough on a floured surface. Scatter the hazelnuts and zest on top of the stretched dough and knead the dough until well combined. Form the dough into a loose ball and put it in a lightly oiled bowl.

4 Cover the bowl with a damp tea towel and leave it to prove in a warm place for up to 2 hours until doubled in size. Meanwhile, line the tin with silicone paper or a double layer of parchment. If using a cake tin, form a collar with the paper 5–10cm (2–4in) higher than the tin.

5 When the dough has doubled in size, knock it back, and stretch it out again. Scatter the chocolate over the surface and bring together, kneading it before shaping it into a round ball. Put it into the tin, cover it again, and leave it to prove for another 2 hours until doubled in size.

6 Preheat the oven to 190°C (375°F/Gas 5). Brush the top of the panettone with beaten egg. Bake in the middle of the oven for 45–50 minutes. Cover the top with foil if it's browning too quickly.

7 Leave to cool in the tin for a few minutes before turning out onto a wire rack to cool completely. The bottom should sound hollow when tapped. Dust with icing sugar to serve.

STORE The panettone will keep in an airtight container for 2 days.

Panettone Bread and Butter Pudding

Any leftover panettone can be turned into this quick and easy dessert. Try introducing different flavours such as orange zest, chocolate, or dried cherries to the dish before baking.

| SERVES 4–6 | 10 MINS | 30–40 MINS |

Ingredients
50g (1¾oz) unsalted butter, softened
250g (9oz) panettone
350ml (12fl oz) single cream or 175ml (6fl oz) double cream and 175ml (6fl oz) milk
2 large eggs
50g (1¾oz) caster sugar
1 tsp vanilla extract

Method

1 Preheat the oven to 180°C (350°F/Gas 4). Use a little of the softened butter to grease a medium sized, shallow baking dish.

2 Slice the panettone into 1cm (½in) thick slices. Butter each slice with a little of the butter and lay them, overlapping slightly, into the baking dish. Whisk together the cream, or cream and milk, eggs, sugar, and vanilla extract. Pour the liquid over the panettone and then gently press down on top to make sure it has all been soaked in the liquid.

3 Bake in the centre of the oven for 30–40 minutes until it is just set, golden brown and puffed up. Serve warm with thick pouring cream.

PREPARE AHEAD Once cooked, this can be stored in the fridge for 3 days. Reheat thoroughly before eating.

ALSO TRY...
Festive Panettone Pudding
Plain panettone can also be spread with a little good-quality marmalade and the cream enriched with 1–2 tbsp whisky and a grating of orange zest and nutmeg, for a festive alternative.

Individual Stuffed Panettones

Try these as an alternative dessert at a Christmas meal.

SERVES 6 | 1 HOUR | 30–35 MINS

Rising, proving, and chilling time
3 hrs rising and proving and 3 hrs chilling

Special equipment
6 x 220g empty food cans, well cleaned
food processor with blade attachment

Ingredients
butter, for greasing
1 quantity panettone dough,
  see page 166, steps 1–9
300g (10oz) mascarpone cheese
300g (10oz) crème fraîche
2 tbsp Kirsch or other fruit liqueur (optional)
12 glacé cherries, quartered
50g (1¾oz) unsalted, shelled pistachio nuts,
  roughly chopped
3 tbsp icing sugar, plus extra for dusting

Method

1 Grease the cans and line them with baking parchment. The parchment should rise to double the height of the cans.

2 Cut the dough into 6 pieces, and place a piece in each can. Cover and leave to rise for 1 hour or until doubled in size. Preheat the oven to 190°C (375°F/Gas 5).

3 Bake for 30–35 minutes. The panettones will be golden-brown. Remove one from its can and tap the base. It should sound hollow. If it does not, remove all of them from their cans, place on a baking tray and bake for 5 minutes. Place on a wire rack and cool.

4 Hollow out the panettones by laying each one on its side and, using a sharp knife and a sawing action, cut a circle in the base 1cm (½in) from the edge. Reserve the disks.

5 Now take the knife and cut down along the insides of the rim nearly to the bottom of the upside down panettone. Neatly hollow out the panettone with your fingers.

6 Put the extracted pieces of the panettone into a food processor and reduce them

to fine breadcrumbs. In a bowl, cream together the mascarpone and crème fraîche with the liqueur (if using). Mix in the breadcrumbs and beat well to combine.

7 Fold through the cherries, pistachios, and icing sugar. Divide the filling between the panettones, pressing it in with the back of a spoon, and cover with the reserved disks.

8 Wrap, and refrigerate for at least 3 hours. Unwrap and dust with icing sugar to serve.

PREPARE AHEAD These will keep overnight in the refrigerator.

BAKER'S TIP
Panettone is an Italian sweet bread traditionally baked for Christmas. Although the process is lengthy, the time taken is mostly for the bread to rise twice. It is not complicated to make and gives a marvellously light result quite unlike a shop-bought panettone.

Bara Brith

This sweet Welsh "speckled bread" is at its best eaten the same day it is made, ideally while still warm and spread with butter.

MAKES 2 LOAVES	40 MINS	25–40 MINS	UP TO 8 WEEKS

Rising and proving time
3–4 hrs

Special equipment
2 x 900g (2lb) loaf tins (optional)

Ingredients
2 tsp dried yeast
250ml (8fl oz) warm milk
60g (2oz) caster sugar,
  plus 2 tbsp for sprinkling
1 egg, beaten
500g (1lb 2oz) strong white bread flour,
  plus extra for dusting
1 tsp salt
60g (2oz) unsalted butter, softened and diced
1 tsp mixed spice
oil, for greasing
225g (8oz) dried mixed fruit
  (raisins, sultanas, and mixed peel)

Method

1 Whisk the yeast into the milk with 1 teaspoon of caster sugar, and leave in a warm place for 10 minutes until the mixture froths. Add most of the beaten egg, reserving a little for glazing.

2 Rub the flour, salt, and butter together until the mixture resembles fine breadcrumbs. Stir in the mixed spice and remaining sugar. Make a well in the centre of the dry ingredients. Pour in the milk mixture, and mix it together with your hands to form a sticky dough.

3 Turn it out onto a lightly floured work surface and knead for up to 10 minutes until soft and pliable but still quite sticky. Add more flour, 1 tablespoon at a time, if it's not forming a ball. Place the dough in a lightly oiled bowl and cover with cling film. Leave it to rise in a warm place for 1½–2 hours until doubled in size.

4 Turn out onto a lightly floured work surface, punch the air out with your fists, and gently stretch to around 2cm (¾in) thick. Scatter the dried fruit over the surface of the dough, and bring it together from the sides into the middle to form a ball again.

5 Now either shape the dough into your desired shape and transfer to a greased baking sheet, or halve and put into the greased loaf tins. Cover with oiled cling film or a clean tea towel, and leave in a warm place to prove for another 1½–2 hours until doubled in size again.

6 Meanwhile, preheat the oven to 190°C (375°F/Gas 5). Brush the bread with a little egg wash and sprinkle it with 1 tablespoon of sugar. Bake for 25–30 minutes for loaf tins, or 35–40 minutes for a large free-form loaf. Cover halfway through cooking time with a piece of foil or baking parchment if it browns too much.

7 The bread is done when it is golden brown, firm to the touch, and the bottom is hollow when tapped. Leave to cool for 20 minutes before cutting, as it will continue to cook after being removed from the oven. Cutting too early causes the steam to escape and the loaf to harden.

STORE The bread will keep in an airtight container for 2 days (see Baker's Tip).

BAKER'S TIP

Baking two loaves at a time and freezing one of them makes good sense when there is lengthy rising and proving to be done. Leftover bread can be toasted for a couple of days after baking, or sliced and used in Bread and Butter Pudding (see page 168).

Cinnamon Rolls

If you prefer, leave the rolls to prove overnight in the fridge (after step 15) and bake in time for a breakfast treat.

MAKES 10–12	40 MINS	25–30 MINS	UP TO 4 WEEKS

Rising and proving time
3–4 hrs or overnight

Special equipment
30cm (12in) round springform cake tin

Ingredients
125ml (4fl oz) milk
100g (3½oz) unsalted butter,
  plus extra for greasing
2 tsp dried yeast
50g (1¾oz) caster sugar
550g (1¼lb) plain flour, sifted,
  plus extra for dusting
1 tsp salt

1 egg, plus 2 egg yolks
vegetable oil, for greasing

For the filling and glaze
3 tbsp cinnamon
100g (3½oz) soft light brown sugar
25g (scant 1oz) unsalted butter,
  melted
1 egg, lightly beaten
4 tbsp caster sugar

1 In a pan, heat 125ml (4fl oz) water, the milk, and butter until just melted. Let it cool.

2 When just warm, whisk in the yeast and a tablespoon of sugar. Cover for 10 minutes.

3 Place the flour, salt, and remaining sugar in a large bowl.

4 Make a well in centre of the dry ingredients and pour in the warm milk mixture.

5 Whisk the egg and egg yolks, and add to the mixture. Combine to form a rough dough.

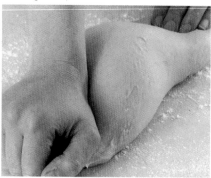

6 Place on a floured surface and knead for 10 minutes. Add extra flour if it's too sticky.

7 Put in an oiled bowl, cover with cling film and keep in a warm place for 2 hours until well risen.

8 Prepare the filling by mixing 2 tablespoons of cinnamon with the brown sugar.

9 When the dough has risen, turn it onto a floured work surface and gently knock it back.

10 Roll it out into a rectangle about 40 x 30cm (16 x 12in). Brush with the melted butter.

11 Scatter with the filling. Leave a 1cm (½in) border on one side and brush it with the egg.

12 Press the filling with the palm of your hand to ensure it sticks to the dough.

13 Roll the dough up, working towards the border. Do not roll too tightly.

14 Cut into 10–12 equal pieces with a serrated knife, taking care not to squash the rolls.

15 Grease and line the tin. Pack in the rolls. Cover and prove for 1–2 hours until well risen.

16 Preheat the oven to 180°C (350°F/Gas 4). Brush with egg and bake for 25–30 minutes.

17 Heat 3 tablespoons water and 2 of sugar until dissolved. Brush the glaze on the rolls.

18 Sprinkle over a mix of the remaining caster sugar and cinnamon, before turning out onto a wire rack to cool. **STORE** The rolls will keep in an airtight container for 2 days.

Sweet Roll variations

Chelsea Buns

These spicy, rolled currant buns were invented in the 18th century at The Bun House in Chelsea, London, where they proved a hit with royalty.

MAKES 9 | 30 MINS | 30 MINS | UP TO 4 WEEKS

Rising and proving time
2 hrs

Special equipment
23cm (9in) round cake tin

Ingredients
1 tsp dried yeast
100ml (3½fl oz) warm milk
280g (10oz) strong white bread flour, sifted, plus extra for dusting
½ tsp salt
2 tbsp caster sugar
45g (1½oz) butter, plus extra for greasing
1 egg, lightly beaten
115g (4oz) mixed dried fruit
60g (2oz) light muscovado sugar
1 tsp mixed spice
clear honey, for glazing

Method
1 Dissolve the yeast in the milk and leave for 5 minutes until frothy. Mix the flour, salt, and caster sugar in a bowl. Rub in 15g (½oz) of the butter. Pour in the egg, followed by the yeasted milk. Mix to form a soft dough. Knead for 5 minutes. Place in a bowl and cover with cling film. Leave in a warm place for 1 hour or until doubled in size.

2 Grease the tin. Tip the dough out onto a lightly floured surface and knead. Roll out to a 30 x 23cm (12 x 9in) rectangle. Melt the remaining butter in a pan over low heat, then brush onto the surface of the dough, leaving a border along the long edges.

3 Mix together the fruit, muscovado sugar, and spice, and scatter over the butter. Roll up the dough from the long edge like a Swiss roll, sealing the end with a little water. Cut the dough into 9 pieces. Place the pieces in the tin and cover with cling film. Leave to prove for up to 1 hour until doubled. Preheat the oven to 190°C (375°F/Gas 5). Bake for 30 minutes, then brush with honey and allow to cool before transferring to a wire rack.

STORE Keep in an airtight container for 2 days.

Spiced Fruit Buns

These sweet buns are simple to make as there is no rolling required.

MAKES 12 | 30 MINS | 15 MINS | UP TO 4 WEEKS

Rising and proving time
1½ hrs

Ingredients
240ml (8fl oz) milk
2 tsp dried yeast
500g (1lb 2oz) strong white bread flour, sifted, plus extra for dusting
1 tsp mixed spice
½ tsp nutmeg
1 tsp salt
6 tbsp caster sugar
60g (2oz) unsalted butter, diced, plus extra for greasing
vegetable oil, for greasing
150g (5½oz) mixed dried fruit
2 tbsp icing sugar
¼ tsp vanilla extract

Method
1 Warm the milk until tepid, stir in the yeast, cover, and leave for 10 minutes until frothy. Place the flour, spices, salt, and sugar in a bowl. Rub in the butter. Add the yeasted milk to form a soft dough. Knead well for 10 minutes. Shape into a ball, then place in a lightly oiled bowl and cover loosely. Leave in a warm place for 1 hour until risen.

2 Tip the dough onto a lightly floured work surface and gently knead in the dried fruit. Divide into 12 pieces, roll into balls, and place, well spaced, on greased baking sheets. Cover loosely and leave in a warm place for 30 minutes or until doubled. Preheat the oven to 200°C (400°F/Gas 6).

3 Bake for 15 minutes or until the buns sound hollow when tapped on the base. Transfer to a wire rack to cool. Meanwhile, combine the icing sugar, vanilla extract, and 1 tablespoon cold water, and brush over the top of the still-warm buns to glaze.

STORE The buns will keep in an airtight container for 2 days.

SWEET BREADS

Hot Cross Buns

These delicious treats are too good to keep just for Easter.

MAKES 10–12 | 30 MINS | 15–20 MINS | UP TO 4 WEEKS

Rising and proving time
2–4 hrs

Special equipment
piping bag with thin nozzle

Ingredients
200ml (7fl oz) milk
50g (1¾oz) unsalted butter
1 tsp vanilla extract
2 tsp dried yeast
100g (3½oz) caster sugar
500g (1lb 2oz) strong white bread flour,
    sifted, plus extra for dusting
1 tsp salt
2 tsp mixed spice
1 tsp cinnamon
150g (5½oz) mixed dried fruit (raisins,
    sultanas, and mixed peel)
1 egg, beaten, plus 1 extra for glazing
vegetable oil, for greasing

For the paste
3 tbsp plain flour
3 tbsp caster sugar

Method

1 Heat the milk, butter, and vanilla in a pan until the butter is just melted. Cool until tepid. Whisk in the yeast and 1 tablespoon of sugar. Cover for 10 minutes until it froths.

2 Put the remaining sugar, flour, salt, and spices into a bowl. Mix in the egg. Add the milk mixture and form a dough. Knead for 10 minutes on a floured surface. Press the dough out into a rectangle, scatter over the dried fruit, and knead briefly to combine.

3 Place in an oiled bowl, cover with cling film, and leave in a warm place for 1–2 hours until doubled. Turn out onto a floured surface, knock it back, divide into 10–12 pieces, and roll into balls. Place them on lined baking sheets. Cover with cling film and leave to prove for 1–2 hours.

4 Preheat the oven to 220°C (425°F/Gas 7). Brush the buns with the beaten egg. For the

paste, mix the flour and sugar with water to make it spreadable. Put it into the piping bag and pipe crosses on the buns. Bake in the top of the oven for 15–20 minutes. Remove to a wire rack and allow to cool for 15 minutes.

STORE Will keep in an airtight container for 2 days.

BAKER'S TIP
These traditional Easter buns are very different and far superior to their bland shop-bought namesakes. They have a delicate, crispy exterior surface and a light, moist, fragrant crumb, with authentically assertive levels of fruit and spice. They are delicious still warm from the oven, spread with cold butter.

Croissants

Although these take some time to make, the final result is well worth the effort. Start a day ahead.

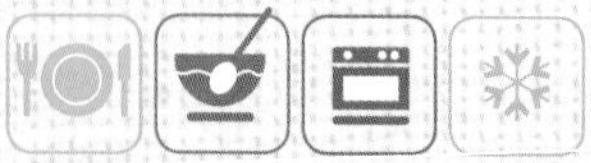

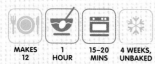

MAKES 12 | 1 HOUR | 15–20 MINS | 4 WEEKS, UNBAKED

Chilling time
5 hrs, plus overnight

Rising time
1 hr

Ingredients

300g (10½oz) strong white bread flour, plus extra for dusting
½ tsp salt
30g (1oz) caster sugar
2½ tsp dried yeast
vegetable oil, for greasing
250g (9oz) unsalted butter, chilled
1 egg, beaten
butter or jam, to serve (optional)

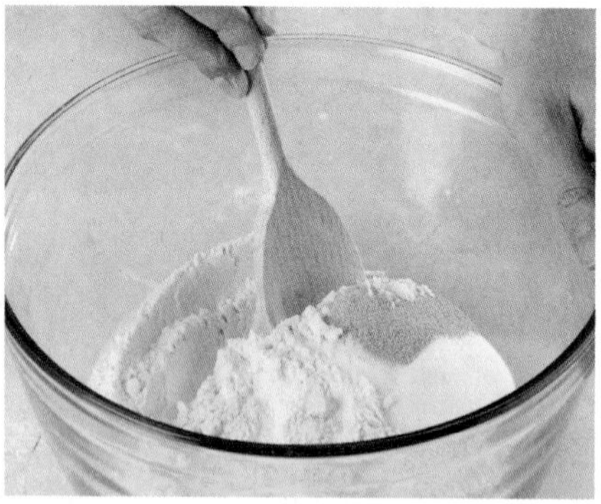

1 Place the flour, salt, sugar, and yeast in a large bowl, and stir to blend well.

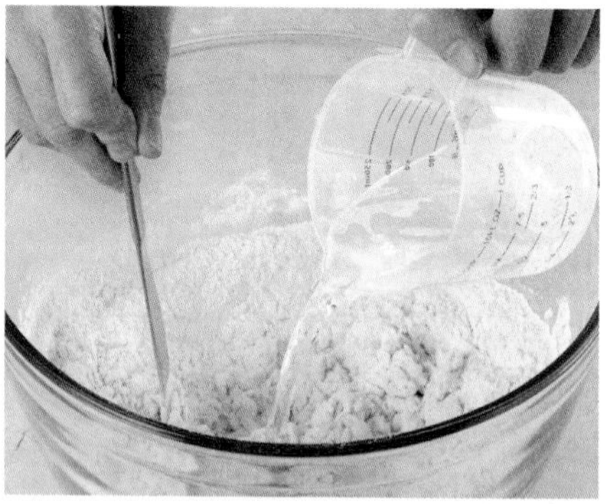

2 Using a table knife, mix in enough warm water, a little at a time, to form a soft dough.

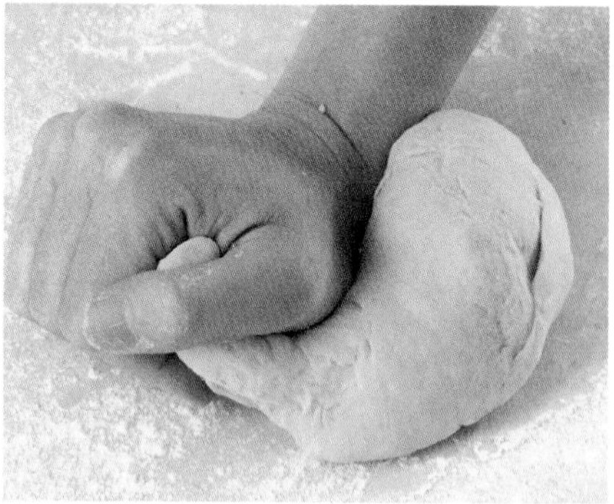

3 Knead on a lightly floured surface until the dough becomes elastic under your hands.

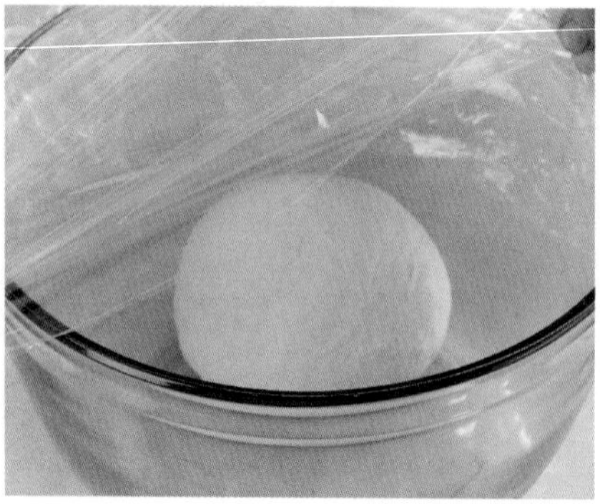

4 Place back in the bowl, cover with lightly oiled cling film, and chill for 1 hour.

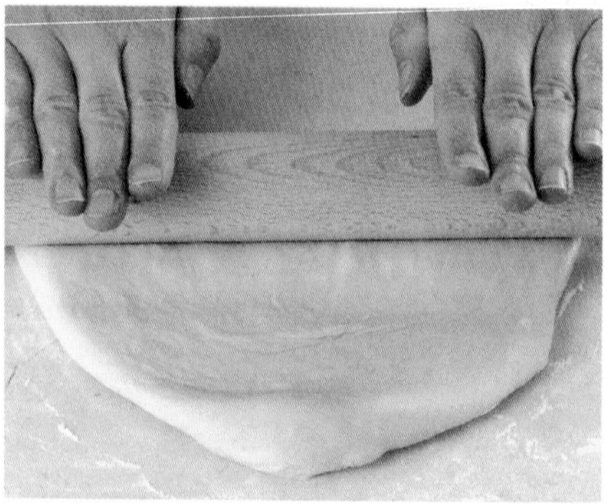

5 Roll the dough out into a rectangle that measures 30 x 15cm (12 x 6in).

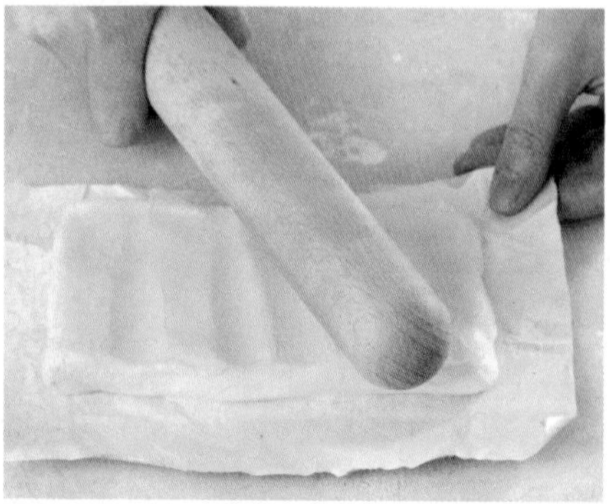

6 Squash the chilled butter with a rolling pin, keeping the pat shape, until 1cm (½in) thick.

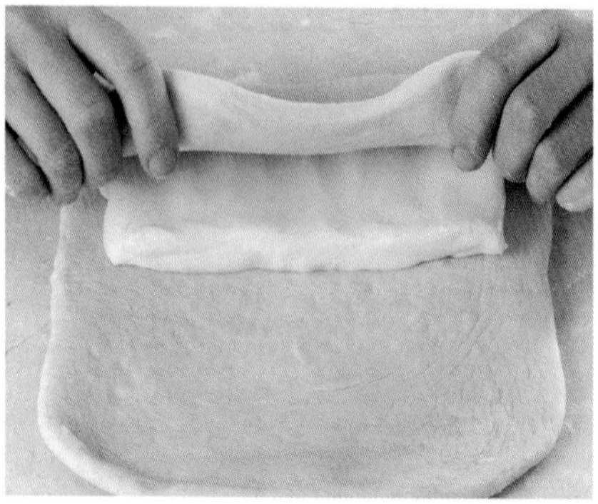

7 Place the butter in the centre of the dough. Fold the dough over it. Chill for 1 hour.

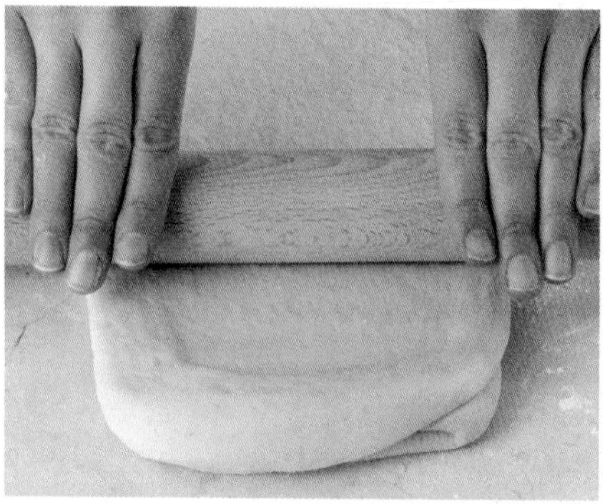

8 Roll out the dough on a lightly floured surface to a 30 x 15cm (12 x 6in) rectangle.

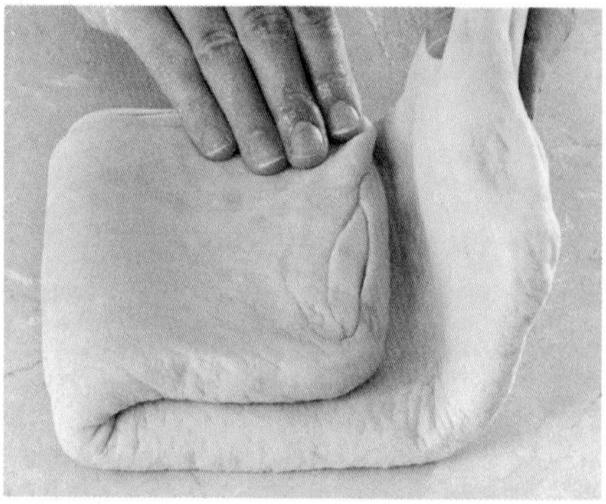

9 Fold the right third to the centre, then the left third over the top. Chill for 1 hour until firm.

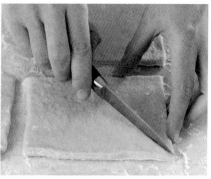

10 Repeat the rolling, folding, and chilling twice. Wrap in cling film and chill overnight.

11 Cut the dough in half and roll out 1 half to a 12 x 36cm (5 x 14½in) rectangle.

12 Cut into 3 x 12cm (1 x 5in) squares, then cut diagonally to make 6 triangles. Repeat.

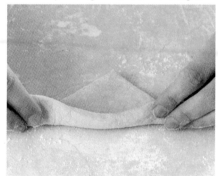

13 Holding the ends of the longest side, roll it towards you. Curve into cresent shapes.

14 Place on baking trays lined with baking parchment, leaving space between each.

15 Cover with lightly oiled cling film. Leave for 1 hour until doubled in size. Remove the film.

16 Preheat the oven to 220°C (425°F/Gas 7). Brush them with egg, then bake for 10 minutes.

17 Reduce the temperature to 190°C (375°F/ Gas 5) and bake for another 5–10 minutes.

STORE The croissants are best served when still warm, with butter and jam, but will keep in an airtight container for 2 days; gently reheat to serve.

Croissant variations

Pains au chocolat

Fresh pains au chocolat, still warm from the oven and oozing with molten chocolate, make the ultimate weekend breakfast treat.

| MAKES 8 | 1 HOUR | 15–20 MINS | UP TO 4 WEEKS |

Chilling time
5 hrs, plus overnight

Rising time
1 hr

Ingredients
1 quantity croissant dough,
  see pages 176–177, steps 1–10
200g (7oz) dark chocolate
1 egg, beaten

Method

1 Divide the dough into 4 equal pieces and roll each out into a rectangle, about 10 x 40cm (4 x 16in). Cut each piece in half, to give 8 rectangles approximately 10 x 20cm (4 x 8in).

2 Cut the chocolate into 16 even-sized strips. Two 100g bars can be easily divided into 8 strips each. Mark each piece of pastry along the long edge at one-third and two-thirds stages.

3 Put a piece of chocolate at the one-third mark, and fold the short end of the dough over it to the two-thirds mark. Now place a second piece of chocolate on top of the folded edge at the two-thirds mark, brush the dough next to it with beaten egg and fold the other side of the dough into the centre, making a triple-layered parcel with strips of chocolate tucked in on either side. Seal all the edges together to prevent the chocolate from oozing out while cooking.

4 Line a baking tray with parchment, place the pastries on it, cover and leave to rise in a warm place for 1 hour until puffed up and nearly doubled in size. Preheat the oven to 220°C (425°F/Gas 7). Brush the pastries with beaten egg and bake in the oven for 10 minutes, then reduce the oven temperature to 190°C (375°F/Gas 5). Bake for another 5–10 minutes, or until golden brown.

STORE The pastries will keep in an airtight container for 1 day.

Cheese and Chorizo Croissants

Spicy chorizo combined with tangy cheese is used here to great effect.

| MAKES 8 | 1 HOUR | 15–20 MINS | UP TO 4 WEEKS |

Chilling time
5 hrs, plus overnight

Rising time
1 hr

Ingredients
1 quantity croissant dough,
  see pages 176–177, steps 1–10
8 slices chorizo, ham, or Parma ham
8 slices cheese, such as Emmental
  or Jarlsberg
1 egg, beaten

Method

1 Divide the dough into 4 equal pieces and roll each out into a rectangle, about 10 x 40cm (4 x 16in). Cut each piece in half, to give 8 rectangles approximately 10 x 20cm (4 x 8in).

2 Place a slice of chorizo or ham on the middle of each croissant and fold one side over it. Place a slice of cheese on the folded over piece, brush with beaten egg and fold the remaining side over it. Seal all the edges. Cover and leave in a warm place for 1 hour or until doubled in size. Preheat the oven to 220°C (425°F/Gas 7).

3 Brush the pastries with egg and bake for 10 minutes, then reduce the temperature to 190°C (375°F/Gas 5). Bake for a further 5–10 minutes or until golden brown.

STORE Keep in an airtight container for 1 day.

BAKER'S TIP
These pastries are endlessly adaptable and can be made with a variety of fillings. Ham and cheese are the most common, but try using a layer of smoked ham and a layer of overlapped chorizo, and sprinkling with smoked paprika, for a more piquant flavour.

Croissants aux amandes

These frangipane-stuffed pastries are light and delicious.

MAKES 12 | 1 HOUR | 15–20 MINS | UP TO 4 WEEKS

Chilling time
5 hrs, plus overnight

Rising time
1 hr

Ingredients
25g (scant 1oz) unsalted butter, softened
75g (2½oz) caster sugar
75g (2½oz) ground almonds
2–3 tbsp milk, if needed
1 quantity croissant dough,
  see pages 176–177, steps 1–10
1 egg, beaten
50g (1¾oz) flaked almonds
icing sugar, to serve

Method

1 For the almond paste, cream the butter and sugar, and blend in the ground almonds. Add milk if the mixture is too thick.

2 Cut the dough into 2 and roll half out on a floured surface to a 12 x 36cm (5 x 14½in) rectangle. Cut into three 12cm (5in) squares, then cut diagonally to make 6 triangles. Repeat to make 6 more triangles.

3 Spread a spoonful of the paste onto each triangle, leaving a 2cm (¾in) border along the 2 longest sides. Brush the borders with egg. Roll the croissant up carefully from the longest side towards the opposite point.

4 Line 2 baking sheets with parchment and place the croissants on them. Cover and leave in a warm place for 1 hour till doubled. Preheat the oven to 220°C (425°F/Gas 7).

5 Brush the croissants with egg. Sprinkle with flaked almonds. Bake for 10 minutes, then reduce the temperature to 190°C (375°F/ Gas 5). Bake for 5–10 minutes until golden. Cool. Dust with icing sugar to serve.

STORE Keep in an airtight container for 1 day.

CROISSANT VARIATIONS

Danish Pastries

Although these deliciously buttery pastries take time to prepare, the home-baked taste is incomparable.

MAKES 18 | 30 MINS | 15–20 MINS | UP TO 4 WEEKS

Chilling time
1 hr

Rising time
30 mins

Ingredients
150ml (5fl oz) warm milk
2 tsp dried yeast
30g (1oz) caster sugar
2 eggs, plus 1 egg for glazing
475g (1lb 1oz) strong white bread
  flour, sifted, plus extra for dusting
½ tsp salt
vegetable oil, for greasing
250g (9 oz) chilled butter
200g (7oz) good-quality cherry,
  strawberry, or apricot jam,
  or compote

1 Mix the milk, yeast, and 1 tablespoon sugar. Cover for 20 minutes, then beat in the eggs.

2 Place the flour, salt, and remaining sugar in a bowl. Make a well and pour in the yeast mix.

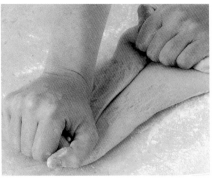

3 Mix the ingredients into a soft dough. Knead for 15 minutes on a floured surface until soft.

4 Place the dough in a lightly oiled bowl, cover with cling film and refrigerate for 15 minutes.

5 On a lightly floured surface, roll the dough out to a square, about 25 x 25cm (10 x 10in).

6 Cut the butter into 3–4 slices, each about 12 x 6 x 1cm (5 x 2½ x ½in).

7 Lay the butter slices on one-half of the dough, leaving a border of 1–2cm (½–¾in).

8 Fold the other half of the dough over the top, pressing the edges with a rolling pin to seal.

9 Generously flour and roll it into a rectangle 3 times as long as it is wide, and 1cm (½in) thick.

10 Fold the top third down into the middle, then the bottom third back over it.

11 Wrap, chill for 15 minutes. Repeat steps 9–10 twice, chilling for 15 minutes each time.

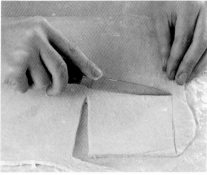

12 Roll onto a floured surface to 5mm–1cm (¼–½in) thick. Cut to 10 x 10cm (4 x 4in) squares.

13 With a sharp knife, make diagonal cuts from each corner to within 1cm (½in) of the centre.

14 Put 1 teaspoon of jam in the centre of each square and fold each corner into the centre.

15 Spoon more jam on the centre, transfer to a lined baking tray, and cover with a tea towel.

16 Leave in a warm place for 30 minutes until risen. Preheat the oven to 200°C (400°F/Gas 6).

17 Brush with egg wash and bake at the top of the oven for 15–20 minutes until golden.

18 Leave to cool slighty then transfer to a wire rack. **STORE** These will keep in an airtight container for 2 days. **PREPARE AHEAD** Make up to end of step 11 and refrigerate overnight.

Danish Pastry variations

Almond Crescents

Butter, sugar, and ground almonds are combined here to make a delicious filling for these light and flaky, crescent-shaped Danish pastries. The pastry can be prepared the night before, ready for rolling.

| MAKES 18 | 30 MINS | 15–20 MINS | UP TO 4 WEEKS |

Chilling time
1 hr

Rising time
30 mins

Ingredients
1 quantity danish pastry dough,
  see pages 180–181, steps 1–11
1 egg, beaten, for glazing
icing sugar, to serve

For almond paste
25g (scant 1oz) unsalted butter, softened
75g (2½oz) caster sugar
75g (2½oz) ground almonds

Method

1 Preheat the oven to 200°C (400°F/Gas 6). Roll half the dough out on a floured surface to a 30cm (12in) square. Trim the edges and cut out nine 10cm (4in) squares. Repeat with the remaining dough.

2 For the almond paste, cream together the butter and caster sugar, then beat in the ground almonds until smooth. Divide the paste into 18 small balls. Roll each one into a sausage shape a little shorter than the length of the dough squares. Place a roll of the paste at one edge of the square, leaving a gap of 2cm (¾in) between it and the edge. Press it down.

3 Brush the clear edge with egg and fold the pastry over the paste, pressing it down. Use a sharp knife to make 4 cuts into the folded edge to within 1½–2cm (½–¾in) of the sealed edge. Transfer to lined baking sheets, cover, and leave in a warm place for 30 minutes, or until puffed. Bend the edges in.

4 Brush with egg and bake in the top third of the oven for 15–20 minutes, until golden brown. Cool. Dust icing sugar over to serve.

STORE The pastries will keep in an airtight container for 2 days.

BAKER'S TIP

Danish pastry recipes often call for the butter to be rolled out between pieces of parchment or bashed with a rolling pin to render it pliable. This is a time-consuming business. Use sliced chilled butter instead, for a fuss-free result.

SWEET BREADS

Cinnamon and Pecan Pinwheels

Try substituting hazelnuts or walnuts here if pecans are unavailable.

MAKES 16	30 MINS	15–20 MINS	UP TO 4 WEEKS

Chilling time
1 hr

Rising time
30 mins

Ingredients
1 quantity danish pastry dough,
  see pages 180–181, steps 1–11
1 egg, beaten, for glazing
100g (3½oz) pecan nuts, chopped
100g (3½oz) soft light brown sugar
2 tbsp cinnamon
25g (scant 1oz) unsalted butter, melted

Method

1 To make the filling, mix the pecans, sugar, and cinnamon. Roll half the dough out on a floured work surface to a 20cm (8in) square. Trim the edges, brush the surface with half the butter and scatter half the pecan mixture over the top, leaving a 1cm (½in) border at the long side that is farthest from you. Brush the border with a little egg.

2 Press the pecan mixture with the palm of your hand to ensure it sticks to the dough. Roll the dough up, starting with the long side and working towards the border. Turn seam-side down. Repeat.

3 Trim the ends and cut each into 8 slices. Turn over and press them to allow the edges to stick. Secure the ends of the dough with a cocktail stick. Line 4 baking sheets with parchment paper. Place 4 pastries on each sheet. Cover and leave in a warm place for 30 minutes, until well puffed up.

4 Preheat the oven to 200°C (400°F/Gas 6). Brush with egg and bake in the top third of the oven for 15–20 minutes until golden.

STORE The pinwheels will keep in an airtight container for 2 days.

Apricot Pastries

The pastry can be prepared the night before, so that 30 minutes of rising in the morning and a quick bake will give you fresh pastries in time for coffee.

MAKES 18	30 MINS	15–20 MINS	UP TO 4 WEEKS

Chilling time
1 hr

Rising time
30 mins

Ingredients
1 quantity danish pastry dough,
  see pages 180–181, steps 1–11
200g (7oz) apricot jam
2 x 400g cans apricot halves

Method.

1 Roll half the dough out on a well-floured work surface to a 30cm (12in) square. Trim the edges and cut out nine 10cm (4in) squares. Repeat with the remaining dough.

2 If the apricot jam has lumps, purée it until smooth. Take 1 tablespoon of jam and, using the back of the spoon, spread it all over a square, leaving a border of about 1cm (½in). Take 2 apricot halves and trim a little off their bottoms if too chunky. Place an apricot half in 2 opposite corners of the square.

3 Take the 2 corners without apricots and fold them into the middle. They should only partially cover the apricot halves. Repeat to fill all the pastries. Place on lined baking sheets, cover, and leave to rise in a warm place for 30 minutes until puffed up. Preheat the oven to 200°C (400°F/Gas 6).

4 Brush the pastries with egg and bake in the top third of the oven for 15–20 minutes until golden. Melt the remaining jam and brush over the pastries, to glaze. Cool for 5 minutes, then transfer to a wire rack.

STORE The pastries will keep in an airtight container for 2 days.

Jam Doughnuts

Doughnuts are surprisingly easy to make. These are light, airy, and taste far nicer than any shop-bought varieties.

MAKES 12 | 30 MINS | 5–10 MINS

Rising and proving time
3–4 hrs

Special equipment
oil thermometer
piping bag with thin nozzle

Ingredients
150ml (5fl oz) milk
75g (2½oz) unsalted butter
½ tsp vanilla extract
2 tsp dried yeast

75g (2½oz) caster sugar
2 eggs, beaten
425g (15oz) plain flour, preferably "00" grade, plus extra for dusting
½ tsp salt
1 litre (1¾ pints) sunflower oil, for deep-frying, plus extra for greasing

For coating and filling
caster sugar, for coating
250g (9oz) good-quality jam (raspberry, strawberry, or cherry), processed until smooth

1 Heat the milk, butter, and vanilla in a pan until the butter melts. Cool until tepid.

2 Whisk in yeast and a tablespoon of sugar. Cover, leave for 10 minutes. Mix in the eggs.

3 Sift the flour and salt into a large bowl. Stir in the remaining sugar.

4 Make a well in the flour and add the milk mixture. Bring together to form a rough dough.

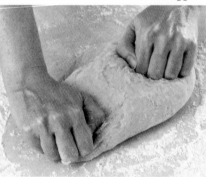

5 Turn the dough onto a floured surface and knead for 10 minutes until soft and pliable.

6 Put in an oiled bowl and cover with cling film. Keep it warm for 2 hours until doubled.

7 On a floured surface, knock back the dough and divide into 12 equal pieces.

8 Roll them between your palms to form balls. Place on baking sheets, spaced well apart.

9 Cover with cling film and a tea towel. Leave in a warm place for 1–2 hours until doubled.

10 Heat a 10cm (4in) depth of oil to 170–180°C (340–350°F), keeping a lid nearby for safety.

11 Slide the doughnuts off the sheets. Do not worry if they are flatter on one side.

12 Carefully lower 3 at a timeinto the hot oil, rounded side down. Turn after 1 minute.

13 Remove with a slotted spoon when golden brown all over. Switch off the heat.

14 Drain on kitchen paper, then, while still hot, toss them in caster sugar. Cool before filling.

15 Put the jam in the piping bag. Pierce each doughnut on the side and insert the nozzle.

16 Gently squirt in about a tablespoon of jam, until it almost starts to spill out again. Dust the hole with a little more sugar, and serve. **STORE** These will keep in an airtight container for 1 day.

Doughnut variations

Ring Doughnuts

Doughnuts are simple to make and home-cooked ones taste delicious. Don't waste the cut-out middles, just fry them separately for a bonus bite-sized treat.

MAKES 12 **35 MINS** **5–10 MINS**

Rising and proving time
3–4 hrs

Special equipment
oil thermometer
4cm (1½in) round pastry cutter

Ingredients
1 quantity doughnut dough,
  see page 184, steps 1–6
1 litre (1¾ pints) sunflower oil, for deep-frying,
  plus extra for greasing
caster sugar, for coating

Method

1 Turn the dough out onto a lightly floured work surface. Gently knock it back, divide into 12, and roll into balls.

2 Place the balls on baking sheets, well apart to allow for them spreading. Cover with cling film and a tea towel, and leave in a warm place for about 1–2 hours until doubled in size.

3 Take a rolling pin and gently flatten the doughnuts to around 3cm (1¼in) in height. Oil the pastry cutter. Cut the centres out and set aside.

4 Pour the oil into a large pan to a depth of at least 10cm (4in) and heat it to 170–180°C (340–350°F). Keep the correct-sized saucepan lid near and do not leave the hot oil unattended. Keep the temperature even, or the doughnuts will burn.

5 Slide the doughnuts off the baking trays using a fish slice. Don't worry if they are flat on one side; they will puff up on cooking. Lower them, rounded-side down, into the hot oil and cook 3 at a time for about 1 minute, turning when the undersides are golden brown.

6 When golden brown all over, remove from the oil with a slotted spoon and drain them on kitchen paper. Turn off the heat when finished frying. The cut-out centres can be fried in a similar way; these are very popular with younger children. While still hot, toss them in caster sugar and leave to cool a little before eating.

STORE These will keep in an airtight container for 1 day.

Custard Doughnuts

Custard is my favourite filling for doughnuts. Use good-quality shop-bought custard here – one that is made with real eggs and plenty of cream.

MAKES 12 **30 MINS** **5–10 MINS**

Proving time
3–4 hrs

Special equipment
oil thermometer
piping bag with thin metal nozzle

Ingredients
1 quantity doughnut dough,
  see page 184, steps 1–6
1 litre (1¾ pints) sunflower oil, for deep-frying,
  plus extra for greasing
caster sugar, for coating
250ml (8fl oz) ready-made custard

Method

1 Turn the dough out onto a lightly floured work surface. Gently knock it back, divide into 12, and roll into balls.

2 Place the balls on baking sheets, well apart to allow for them spreading. Cover lightly with cling film and a tea towel, and leave in a warm place for 1–2 hours until almost doubled in size.

3 Pour the oil into a large, heavy saucepan to a depth of at least 10cm (4in) and heat it to 170–180°C (340–350°F). Keep the correct-sized saucepan lid nearby and never leave the hot oil unattended. Regulate the temperature, making sure it remains even, or the doughnuts will burn.

4 Slide the risen doughnuts off the baking trays using a fish slice. Do not worry if they are flatter on one side; they will puff up on cooking. Lower them, rounded-side down, into the hot oil and cook 3 at a time for about 1 minute, turning as soon as the undersides are golden brown. When golden brown on all sides, turn off the heat, remove the doughnuts from the oil with a slotted spoon and drain them on kitchen paper.

5 While hot, toss them in caster sugar and leave to cool. To fill the doughnuts, place the custard in the piping bag and pierce each doughnut on the side. Make sure the nozzle goes into the centre of the doughnut. Squirt a tablespoon of custard into the doughnut, until it almost starts to spill out. Dust the hole with sugar to disguise it.

STORE These will keep in an airtight container for 1 day.

Churros

These cinnamon- and sugar-sprinkled Spanish snacks take minutes to make and will be devoured just as quickly. Try them dipped in hot chocolate.

SERVES
2–4

10 MINS

5–10 MINS

Special equipment
oil thermometer
piping bag with 2cm (¾in) nozzle

Ingredients
25g (scant 1oz) unsalted butter
200g (7oz) plain flour
50g (1¾oz) caster sugar
1 tsp baking powder
1 litre (1¾ pints) sunflower oil, for deep-frying
1 tsp cinnamon

Method

1 Measure 200ml (7fl oz) boiling water into a jug. Add the butter and stir until it melts. Sift together the flour, half the sugar, and the baking powder into a bowl.

2 Make a well in the centre and slowly pour in the hot butter liquid, beating continuously, until you have a thick paste; you may not need all the liquid. Leave the mixture to cool and rest for 5 minutes.

3 Pour the oil into a large, heavy-based saucepan to a depth of at least 10cm (4in) and heat it to 170–180°C (340–350°F). Keep the correct-sized saucepan lid nearby and never leave the hot oil unattended. Regulate the temperature, making sure it remains even, or the churros will burn.

4 Place the cooled mixture into the piping bag. Pipe 7cm (scant 3in) lengths of the dough into the hot oil, using a pair of scissors to snip off the ends. Do not crowd the pan, or the temperature of the oil will go down. Cook the churros for 1–2 minutes on each side, turning them when they are golden brown.

5 When done, remove the churros from the oil with a slotted spoon and drain on kitchen paper. Switch off the heat.

6 Mix the remaining sugar and the cinnamon together on a plate and toss the churros in the mixture while still hot. Leave to cool for 5–10 minutes before serving while still warm.

STORE These will keep in an airtight container for 1 day.

BAKER'S TIP

Churros can be made in only a few minutes, making them an almost instant treat. The batter can be enriched with egg yolk, butter, or milk, but the basic quantities of liquid to dry ingredients should be maintained. The thinner the batter, the lighter the results, but frying with a liquid batter takes a little practice.

Index

About the author

After spending years as an international model, Caroline Bretherton dedicated herself to her passion for food, founding her company, Manna Food, in 1996.

Her fresh, light, and stylish cooking soon developed a stylish following to match, with a catering clientele that included celebrities, art galleries, theatres, and fashion magazines, as well as cutting edge businesses. She later expanded the company to include an all-day eatery called Manna Café on Portobello Road, in the heart of London's Notting Hill.

A move into the media has seen her working consistently in television over the years, guesting on and presenting a wide range of food programmes for terrestrial and cable broadcasters.

More recently Caroline has worked increasingly in print, becoming a regular contributor to *The Times on Saturday,* and writing her first book *The Allotment Cookbook.*

In her spare time, Caroline tends her beloved allotment near her home in London, growing a variety of fruits, vegetables, and herbs. When she can, she indulges her passion for wild food foraging, both in the city and the country.

She is married to Luke, an academic, and has two boys, Gabriel and Isaac, who were more than happy to test the recipes for this book.

Acknowledgments

The author would like to thank
Mary-Clare, Dawn, and Alastair at Dorling Kindersley for their help and encouragement with this massive task, as well as Borra Garson and all at Deborah McKenna for all their work on my behalf. Lastly I would like to thank all my family and friends for their tremendous encouragement and appetites!

Dorling Kindersley would like to thank
The following people for their work on the photoshoot:

Art Directors
Nicky Collings, Miranda Harvey, Luis Peral, Lisa Pettibone

Props Stylist
Wei Tang

Food Stylists
Kate Blinman, Lauren Owen, Denise Smart

Home Economist Assistant
Emily Jonzen

Baking equipment used in the step-by-step photography kindly donated by Lakeland. For all your baking needs contact: www.lakeland.co.uk; or order by phone on 015394 88100.

Caroline de Souza for art direction and setting the style of the presentation stills photography.

Dorothy Kikon for editorial assistance and Anamica Roy for design assistance.

Jane Ellis for proofreading and Susan Bosanko for indexing.

Thanks to the following people for their work on the US edition:

Consultant
Kate Curnes
Americanizers
Nichole Morford and Jenny Siklós

Thanks also to Steve Crozier for retouching.